Sometimes
MIRRORS

LIE

and other stories
to inspire wisdom
and courage

ISBN: 978-1-950791-51-4

Illustrations by Igor Kondratyuk

Cover art by Kristi Yoder

Cover and text layout design: Kristi Yoder

Published by:
TGS International
P.O. Box 355
Berlin, Ohio 44610 USA
Phone: 330.893.4828
Fax: 330.893.2305
www.tgsinternational.com

Sometimes
MIRRORS

LIE

and other stories
to inspire wisdom
and courage

Faythelma Bechtel

Dedication

I dedicate this book to all the children in our family (now grown adults with families) who lived and illustrated the book of Proverbs in many practical ways—especially to Matthew who provided the foundation and lessons learned in a number of these stories.

Acknowledgments

I thank God first of all for the book of Proverbs and the many lessons it teaches.

I also thank God for the many children in my life who gave occasion for some of these stories.

A special thanks to Marie Latta, a writer friend I met over 50 years ago in Battle Creek, Michigan, at a series of writing classes. Through the years we kept contact by letters and now by email. She contributed a number of true stories.

Also, I thank James Beachy, Carol Bechtel (my daughter-in-law), and Sabrina and Shaylyn Miller (my granddaughters). Your stories all added meaning and variety to the book. Thank you for your contributions.

A special thank you goes to Shanda Good, my TGS editor.

Thank you, Shanda, for all your guidance, help, and patience. And thanks to TGS for printing the book and making it available to the children of our world. May the lessons help shape the lives of the readers, and may they find refuge and instruction in the book of Proverbs. May they put away foolishness and grow in godly wisdom.

Blessings of love and prayers,
Faythelma Bechtel

Table of Contents

Introduction

Many of these stories are true. They are about real boys and girls with real troubles and real behavior problems. Some of these boys and girls lived in our home under foster care, and five were adopted into our family. My husband and I learned from many good times in our home—and from many difficult situations. Foster care and adoption places a family in the public eye. It opens the home for much more criticism than the family expects or wants.

Some of the stories took place in a public school in Michigan before there were many Christian day schools available. The stories by Marie Latta are from a Christian but non-Anabaptist background.

Remember, God loves you and gave you the parents you need

to help direct your footsteps from earth to heaven. By listening to your parents and obeying them, you will make life more enjoyable for them and for yourself, and your behavior will be pleasing to God.

It is my prayer that you will learn from the mistakes of the children in these stories and follow the good example of those who learned important lessons.

—Faythelma Bechtel

Sometimes Mirrors Lie

Luella pushed open the church door and stepped outside with her friend Katelyn.

"Have you ever watched Jewel walk back and forth in front of that long mirror in the girls' restroom?" Luella asked. "She must really think she's a beautiful jewel! She always looks so pleased with herself."

"Yes, the way she struts around makes me sick. She isn't the only girl with blond hair and blue eyes," Katelyn replied. "But talking about her doesn't really make me any better than she is. After today's sermon, I think I need to work on getting beauty on the inside rather than being so concerned about the outside. I need to work on building character."

"I guess talking about another person isn't a way to build

good character," Luella laughed. "I really wonder what she has to say about us."

"That really isn't important, is it? What God sees inside me and what He thinks of me is the most important, isn't it?" Katelyn said.

"Yes, you're right again," Luella answered as she joined her family to leave for home. "See you this evening for chorus practice."

At the dinner table Katelyn's mother asked, "Can you tell me what the sermon was about? Since I was at home feeling sick I would like to hear what you learned."

"Brother James said girls are most interested in beauty and fellows are interested in strength," Trenton offered. "But I'd say we fellows don't go around trying to show off our strength like the girls try to show off their beauty."

"You boys are always having some kind of strength contest," Katelyn replied. "Oh, come on, Trenton, we girls don't show off."

"Some of them do, and you are always looking at that little mirror in your purse," Trenton teased.

Katelyn's face reddened. Why didn't looking in a small mirror seem as bad as marching in front of a long mirror?

"I didn't ask for a debate," Mother interrupted. "I would like to know what the sermon was about. What was the title?"

Father spoke up, "The title was 'Sometimes Mirrors Lie,' and the text was Proverbs 31:30. 'Favour is deceitful, and beauty is vain: but a woman that feareth the LORD, she shall be praised.' It was a sermon especially for youth.

"Brother James said true beauty isn't what you see in the

mirror. True beauty does not come from what you put *on* but from what you put *in* your heart and mind. He gave us a list of things that will help develop character and make us beautiful and strong on the inside."

Katelyn jumped up from the table and brought her Bible from the living room. "I took notes and I have the list," she said. "Do you want to hear the ones that stood out to me the most?"

"Sure," Mother replied.

So Katelyn began:

- Obedience—willingly and promptly doing what I am asked to do
- Respect—holding others' opinions higher than my own
- Cheerfulness—being happy and looking at the bright side even when things don't go my way
- Kindness—seeing the needs of others and reaching out to help them
- Contentment—being grateful and accepting that what God has given or allowed is enough
- Truthfulness—being open and transparent, with nothing in my life to hide

"He mentioned more than these, and many more could be added, but these will keep me busy for quite a while," Katelyn said. "I really need to work on developing my character."

"Good for you," Trenton applauded, then more soberly added, "I think I could do some work on my inside too."

"I am still curious about the sermon title. How do mirrors

lie?" Mother asked.

"Well, when I stand in front of the mirror with my muscle flexed, I appear strong," Trenton said. "But God sees inside and tells me I'm not strong when I give in to watching something I should not look at, or when I read a book that doesn't help me to be a better person—or when I listen to the wrong music," Trenton finished with his head down.

"Well, son, it does sound as though you have some work to do to build those conscience and wisdom muscles," Father replied. "But admitting things goes a long way toward finding victory."

"And you, Katelyn, does the mirror ever lie to you?" Mother asked.

"Yes, it does," Katelyn answered with downcast eyes. "On Sunday mornings when I'm dressed for church, I look kind of pretty and I am pleased with myself. I really feel like a good Christian. But other times the mirror shows an angry face, a frustrated face, or a very unhappy face. The mirror isn't lying to me then, but my heart tries to lie to me, making me think I am still pretty. But God sees the inside and that is not very pretty."

"It sounds as though you heard a very good sermon, and we all have some work to do. We want to help you children develop godly character that is truly beautiful," Mother said.

"Then Brother James read a short clipping about Fanny Crosby," Father said. "I asked him for a copy of it so I could read it to you, dear." And Father read aloud:

Fanny Crosby was born in a one-story cottage. She never remembered her father, for he died when she was twelve months old. Fanny was born a perfect and

Sometimes Mirrors Lie

beautiful baby, but when she was six weeks old, she caught a slight cold in her eyes. A country doctor, who was a stranger to the family, was called in to treat her. He prescribed hot mustard poultices to be applied to her eyes, and that destroyed her sight completely. It was later learned that the man was not qualified to practice medicine, but he had left town and was never heard of again.

> Favour is deceitful, and beauty is vain: but a woman that feareth the LORD, she shall be praised.
> Proverbs 31:30

Fanny was not pretty with those blind eyes and her blindness was a handicap, but she never felt resentment against the doctor. She believed her loss of sight was permitted by the Lord to fulfill His plan for her life. She had a beautiful attitude, a true result of her inner beauty.

At the age of eight Fanny wrote the attitude of her life. This is her first recorded poetry.

O what a happy soul am I! Although I cannot see,
I am resolved that in this world, contented I will be.
How many blessings I enjoy, that other people don't;
To weep and sigh because I'm blind, I cannot and I won't!

Fanny is remembered as the greatest hymn writer of the Christian church. She "saw" over 8,000 of her poems set to music and more than 100 million copies of her songs printed.

"I think it is a great pity that the Master did not give you sight when He showered so many other gifts upon you," remarked one well-meaning preacher.

Fanny Crosby responded at once, as she had heard such comments before. "Do you know that if at birth I had been able to make one petition, it would have been that I was born blind?" she said. "Because when I get to heaven, the first face that shall ever gladden my sight will be that of my Savior."

Fanny proved what it was to be beautiful from the inside out. Fanny's work has been praised, while her work praised the Lord.

"Why don't we look in one of our hymn books and see how many of Fanny's hymns we can find?" Father suggested.

"And when we look in the mirror, we can remember Fanny's blind eyes and lovely character," Mother added.

2

Wisdom—God's Gift

"There are countless books in this world, some terrible, some bad, some good, and some wonderful. You can't possibly read all of them, so fill your mind with only the very best." Wilma listened carefully as Brother David admonished the believers. "There are many, perhaps countless, songs and kinds of music; you can't possibly sing or listen to them all. So listen to and sing only the best.

"You are free to choose," Brother David went on from his place behind the pulpit, "but always remember, you are not free from the consequences of your choices. When you choose bad books and wrong music, you are putting poison into your brain and body; there will be consequences. Your decisions determine your destiny.

"I want to challenge you young people especially. Read the book of Proverbs and learn about God's wisdom and the way to live a life pleasing to Him. In James 1:5, God promises, 'If any of you lack wisdom, let him ask of God, that giveth to all men liberally, and upbraideth not; and it shall be given him.' Ask God for the wisdom to make the right choices."

The church service ended with the usual friendly fellowship. At home around the dinner table with her family, Wilma announced, "I want to begin reading through the book of Proverbs as Brother David suggested."

"I think that is a good thing for you to do," Dad replied with a special smile at Wilma. "The book of Proverbs is full of wisdom for everyday living. You might want to mark all the wisdom words."

"What do you mean, Dad? Write in my Bible? And how do I know what are wisdom words?" Wilma asked.

"What I mean is, mark with a colored pencil all the words like *wisdom, wise, wisely,* and *wiser.* Then when you are reading, those words will stand out. You also could mark all the fool's words with a different color. Proverbs speaks much about *the fool, fools, foolish,* and *foolishness.* You may want to use the *Strong's Concordance.*"

> For the Lord giveth wisdom: out of his mouth cometh knowledge and understanding.
> Proverbs 2:6

"Oh, thanks, Dad. I like that idea. I think I will begin this afternoon. Is the concordance in your office?" Wilma asked as she helped clear the table.

On Monday evening during family worship, Dad asked Wilma, "Well, how about a report on what you have found in Proverbs?"

"I have only done the wisdom words so far," Wilma answered. "There are so many!"

"Yes, tell us how many of each you found," Mom urged. "I'm anxious to hear."

"Ah, here's my paper in my Bible," Wilma said.

"*Wisdom* is used 54 times; *wise*, 65 times; *wisely*, 3 times; and *wiser*, only 2 times. That makes a total of 124 'wisdom' words—more than in any other book of the Bible."

"Good job," Dad said. "The book of Proverbs is truly a book of wisdom. Proverbs 2:6 tells us that God gives wisdom and from His mouth comes knowledge and understanding. That is why His Word—the Bible—is so important. In ourselves, we do not have the wisdom, knowledge, and understanding we need to live in this challenging world.

"What are some things that make life challenging for you, Wilma?" Dad asked kindly.

"Well, what to read and listen to have been a challenge, but since Brother David's sermon, I want to read and listen to only the best—and to leave all the rest. Just this afternoon I stopped by the drug store for cough drops, and I stopped and looked at the books on the rack. I started looking at those Amish love stories and was shocked at some of the scenes written in them. I thought they were supposed to be Christian books. Suddenly I remembered the words, 'Read only the best' and I closed the book."

"What is it about those books that attracts you, Wilma?" Mom asked.

"Well, the stories sound so exciting. The girl is always beautiful and the fellows handsome and courageous . . . but are they truly Christian? I decided they aren't the best for me to read. I want to read about real people, not people from someone's imagination."

"That sounds like a very good decision," Mom replied. "But the devil is always out there trying to draw you away from your good determinations. And he even uses so-called 'Christian books' that are full of wrong ideas and choices. Beauty and handsome looks are not what pleases the Lord. Love stories fill a girl's mind with all kinds of false notions about what will truly fulfill you."

Wilma looked thoughtful. Then she said, "Another real challenge I have is Foolish Frank at school. He is always picking on me."

"Why do you call him foolish?" Dad asked.

"Oh, that's a nickname most of us call him," Wilma said, her face reddening. "He is always doing and saying such foolish things."

"I wonder how wise it is to remind him of his foolishness all the time. Maybe if you just called him Frank, he would behave better," Mom suggested.

"I will try to remember that, Mom. But he often calls me Wise Wilma. He says I'm always preaching to him and that I think I am wise," Wilma explained.

"Perhaps you are coming across as self-righteous. I'm sure

you want to stand for only what is right, but there is always a conflict between foolishness and wisdom. Maybe you need to talk less and instead show more of Christ's love," Dad said.

"Sounds like a good idea," Wilma replied. "Truly, I don't want to appear self-righteous."

"Well, it's time to say good night. Perhaps by Thursday night you can tell us about the 'foolish' words you found," Dad suggested.

"Yes, I will do that," Wilma answered.

Thursday night soon arrived and Wilma had her list ready. After Dad shared from Matthew 5 for devotions, he asked Wilma, "Are you ready to report on the 'foolish' words in Proverbs?"

"Yes, I am. The word *fool* appears 37 times. There are 23 *fools* or *fool* with an apostrophe and s. The word *foolish* is used 13 times; *foolishly*, 2 times; and *foolishness*, 8 times. That makes a total of 83 'foolish' words in Proverbs—more than in any other book of the Bible."

"Thank you, Wilma. I think that was a very worthwhile study," Dad said.

"I think so too," Wilma replied. "Thanks for prompting me to do it."

Sorrow—The Better Path?

"Oh, I wish Mom could be there to speak at my graduation lunch. I—I wish . . . but . . ." Shaylyn's voice faltered to a stop as she looked up at Grandma Bechtel.

It was April, and Shaylyn Miller and two other girls would soon graduate from eighth grade. Their mothers and older sisters were giving a lunch in their honor. But Shaylyn's mother was very ill from cancer, and she was not able to go away from home very often.

"I know that is your heart's desire, Shay, but it may not be the best for your mother," Grandma said quietly. "She is very weak."

Shaylyn watched as Grandma mixed meatloaf for supper. Grandma had come from her home in Oregon to Missouri several times in the past few months to help out. But Shaylyn realized that Grandma too was struggling. They had been through so much in the last few years. First it had been Great Grandma who died, then Aunt Cynthia, and then Grandpa Bechtel. And now Mom, Grandma's daughter Sonya, was slipping away. Sometimes it seemed that sorrow would destroy their family. How could Grandma bear another loss? How would *any* of them bear it?

Shaylyn looked up at Grandma hopefully. "Maybe *you* could come to the lunch . . . if Mom can't come."

> Ponder the path of thy feet, and let all thy ways be established.
> Proverbs 4:26

Grandma looked perplexed. How does a grandmother ever take a mother's place? Impossible! Grandma didn't know what to say. She gladly helped with the laundry, the cooking, the cleaning, and the story reading. But this was different. It seemed God was asking too much.

"It won't be easy for me, Shaylyn . . . but—but I will try," Grandma said. And she did. At the graduation lunch Grandma spoke a few words of encouragement. Then with a tremulous voice and tears pushing at her eyes she read a poem by Robert Frost:

The Road Not Taken

Two roads diverged in a yellow wood,
And sorry I could not travel both
And be one traveler, long I stood
And looked down one as far as I could
To where it bent in the undergrowth;

Then took the other, as just as fair,
And having perhaps the better claim,
Because it was grassy and wanted wear;
Though as for that the passing there
Had worn them really about the same,

And both that morning equally lay
In leaves no step had trodden black.
Oh, I kept the first for another day!
Yet knowing how way leads on to way,
I doubted if I should ever come back.

I shall be telling this with a sigh
Somewhere ages and ages hence:
Two roads diverged in a wood, and I—
I took the one less traveled by,
And that has made all the difference.

Shaylyn looked at Grandma, her face expectant but sad. It seemed Grandma was saying, *Oh, Shaylyn. Your dear mother has taken the road less traveled and is on the path toward earthly death—but eternal life. It is very painful for all of us. We want to rejoice with her, but it will be such a huge job to fill her place. And as the oldest daughter, much of it will fall on you.*

Aloud, Grandma said, "You girls, Shaylyn, Dawn, and Brenda, are on the threshold of new opportunities and bigger challenges. You have completed eighth grade, but there is much more ahead. Your parents have taught you and led you into the right path, and now it is up to you to make the right choices.

Remember, your choices will make a difference, both now and in eternity. God has promised to direct your paths when you trust Him and allow Him to help you choose what is right. He will be there for you—always."

Shaylyn remembered Grandma's words during the coming weeks. Only a few weeks later her mother slipped into eternity. Mom's suffering was over. But her family was left behind in sorrow.

o o o o o o o o o o o o o o o

Shaylyn heard her little sister's sobs as the back door banged and footsteps crossed the kitchen. She hurried to meet her sister Sabrina, who was carrying Shanita. Dad got there first.

"Shhh, Shanita. Tell us what's wrong," Dad comforted. But three-year-old Shanita was crying too hard to talk.

"She fell off the swing," Sabrina said.

A fierce protectiveness welled up in Shaylyn as she reached for her little sister and held her close. *I will be here to comfort you, Shanita. No matter what!*

Caring for her little sister gave Shaylyn focus in the difficult days and weeks that followed. Someone needed her.

Her family needed her too. Cooking, laundry, cleaning, packing lunches, combing her little sisters' hair, cleaning her brother's room, ironing Dad's shirts—sometimes the tasks seemed endless. She often found it hard to encourage her siblings to help with the work without being too bossy.

Many times that summer, Shaylyn buried herself in a book.

Sometimes Mirrors Lie

Reading gave some reprieve from the ache in her heart and the troubled thoughts swirling in her mind. Often she swallowed the tears and put on a brave smile for her family. But at night, alone in her room when the others were asleep, she allowed the tears to flow. Sometimes they brought relief. But at other times Shaylyn gave in to self-pity. She felt as though the weight of the world were on her shoulders.

> I have taught thee in the way of wisdom; I have led thee in right paths. Proverbs 4:11

But there were bright spots too. The ladies from their church stopped in sometimes to cheer the family and to answer questions that only a woman could answer. One family helped Shaylyn and her sisters can tomato products. More than once Shaylyn opened a cookbook and found a note of encouragement from a relative. Dad's cousin spent Thanksgiving with them, bringing companionship, cheer, and advice.

The songs in church touched Shaylyn and at times she fought tears. People did not mention Mom as often anymore, but Shaylyn knew that God had not forgotten. He could see her pain. He cared and understood more than anyone else. He was the best comforter.

The words from 2 Corinthians 1:4 took on new meaning for Shaylyn. "Who comforteth us in all our tribulation, that we may be able to comfort them which are in any trouble, by the comfort wherewith we ourselves are comforted of God." Because of her own sorrow, she was able to reach out to others with empathy, and somehow that was healing to her own heart.

Shaylyn began to understand that her mother's death had caused her to think seriously about life. She was learning to depend more on God, and to talk to Him in her thoughts throughout the day as she went about her work. God was helping her to trust Him and leave the *whys* in His hands.

And then Janice came. A new mother did not fill the exact spot that Shaylyn's own mother had, but she was a friend. She was there for Dad. And she took over many of the household duties that Shaylyn had done for two years. Shaylyn once more found herself rollicking with her siblings around the house and in the yard. For months she had been too bowed down with trouble to allow herself to have fun. Now she felt more carefree.

Shaylyn still thinks of her mother and wishes she could talk to her at times. She often thinks of Grandma and her example of faithfulness in the face of loss after loss. With the help of God, a loving family, and many friends they made it through those first difficult years. Shaylyn's sorrow has made her—not bitter—but better.

—Shaylyn Miller

4

Climbing Carl and His Kite

"Carl, I told you not to climb that cherry tree. Some of the branches are dying and getting weak."

"But Mom, I love to sway back and forth on them!" Carl exclaimed.

Mom's eyes grew big. "Carl, do I need to watch you like a three-year-old? I have told you time and again not to swing on the branches of that old tree. See all the broken branches under it. It seems to be a branch-shedding tree . . . if there is such a thing," she said, laughing. "It's just a weak tree and there are other trees you can climb."

Dad entered the room just then. "You listen to your mother," he said. "Proverbs says a wise person will hear instruction, but a fool does not listen."

"I hear you, Mom," Carl said with a lopsided grin.

"You may hear me, but are you really listening? When you really listen, you will follow my instructions."

"I will try to hear and listen better," Carl promised. "May I go now?"

Soon Carl was high in the oak tree behind the house. This was his favorite pastime. From there he could watch what his neighbors were doing in their backyards.

There was Mrs. Horst hanging out baby diapers. And Carl could smell barbecue. Someone was cooking supper on the grill tonight. He looked to his right and then to his left. Sure enough! There was the grill and the cook. Mr. Harper was flipping something onto the grill; it smelled like barbecued chicken. He wished his family would cook out more often, but Dad often got home too late and Mother had supper ready inside.

From his perch Carl could see Tony and Teddy, the Mattson twins, playing with a big green ball. Mrs. Mattson was working in her flower bed, and there was Taffy, their cat, digging in the other end of the flower bed. Suddenly Mrs. Mattson jumped up and chased the cat away. Carl laughed. How he enjoyed watching people from his perch! He knew what his neighbors were doing, but his neighbors did not know what he was doing. That gave him a feeling of importance.

The next day was Saturday, and after breakfast Carl started on his weekly job, mowing the lawn. It was a beautiful, sunny day, and as Carl pushed the mower back and forth he noticed a breeze picking up. *Hey, maybe I could fly my new kite today,* he thought. *That'll be fun!*

When the lawn mowing was finished, Carl carefully put his kite together and soon had it ready to fly. He was carrying it toward the field when Mother opened the door and called out, "Carl, be sure to stay away from the cherry tree. You don't want to get your kite caught in it. Can you hear me?"

"Yes, I hear you," Carl called back. "I am listening." He sighed. How often had he heard those instructions?

Soon the kite was high in the sky. Carl almost felt like he could fly with it. Gazing dreamily at his kite, he remembered a poem he used to say,

> One little kite in the sky so blue.
> Along came another, then there were two.
> Two little kites flying high above me.
> Along came another, then there were three.
> Three little kites, just watch how they soar.
> Along came another, then there were four.
> Four little kites, so high and so alive.
> Along came another, then there were five.
> Five little kites dancing 'cross the sky.
> What a sight to see, way up so high![1]

And his mother would add these lines,

> With wisdom in your heart, you will fly the right direction.
> With foolishness in the mind, you have not God's protection.

It would be fun to have others flying kites with him, but then

---

[1] This poem is usually attributed to Jean Warren.

the kites could get tangled and that would be a mess.

Suddenly there was a change in the wind and the kite began tumbling downward. It seemed headed for the cherry tree. *Oh, no! I should have been paying more attention to my kite instead of thinking about that poem.*

Dismayed, Carl looked up at his kite caught in the cherry tree. It wasn't caught very high. Maybe if he was really careful

Sometimes Mirrors Lie

he could climb up and get it. Maybe he could prove to Mom the tree wasn't as weak as she thought. All thoughts of playmates, wisdom, and foolishness vanished.

He ran to the tree and began climbing. Just a little higher and he would have it. But as he stretched to reach the kite, he heard a loud *crack*. Suddenly he found himself falling, hitting branches on the way down. He hit the ground with a thud, and several small branches landed on top of him. "Ouch! Oh!" he groaned as he stared up at his kite. "Help!"

How his arm hurt! He had tried to catch himself with his right arm, and now it hurt terribly. He lay there in pain, afraid to move.

Soon his mother was standing over him. "Carl! Are you hurt badly?" she asked anxiously. "I thought I heard you yell. Here, let me help you up."

"No, no! Don't touch my right arm," Carl cried. "Take hold of my left arm." He managed to get to his feet and move slowly toward the house.

"Oh, I think we need to go to the ER. By the looks of that angle in your arm, I'm sure you have a broken bone," Mother said.

On the way to the hospital, Carl did some serious thinking. As he trembled with pain, he tried to gather his thoughts. He had heard his mother warn him many times about that "weak tree." Why hadn't he believed her? Hadn't Dad talked about a verse in Proverbs that said something about listening to instruction and becoming wise? He certainly hadn't acted very wisely when he climbed into that tree. He had acted very foolishly.

Finally Carl said, "You know, Mom, I heard you say, 'Stay

away from that tree,' and I heard you say, 'Never climb that tree.' I heard you with my ears but I did not listen with my heart. I'm sorry for not listening. This arm will be my reminder for a long time."

Hear instruction, and be wise, and refuse it not. Blessed is the man that heareth me, watching daily at my gates, waiting at the posts of my doors. For whoso findeth me findeth life, and shall obtain favour of the Lord. Proverbs 8:33-35

5

What Is Strength?

"Hey, Sam, let's arm wrestle."

Wendy and Elyse walked out of the school building just in time to hear Darren's loud challenge.

"Boys are so disgusting," Wendy said in a low voice as the girls headed away from the picnic table where the boys had gathered. "They are always trying to prove who is the strongest. Looks like there is going to be another arm wrestling match."

"Well, Darren is especially disgusting. He's such a bragger!" Elyse exclaimed. "But I sort of like to watch them arm wrestle when they don't pay attention to us watching."

"Yeah, me too," Wendy admitted. "Let's move over where we can see and hear better and they can't see us so well."

"Come on, Sam, I'll arm wrestle you and beat you!" Darren

challenged again.

"No thanks, I don't want to arm wrestle," Sam replied.

"You're a scaredy-cat. You know I'll beat you," declared Darren.

"No, I know you won't play fair," Sam stated.

"Of course I'll play fair. I always play fair," Darren said with a grin. "Come on, Sam, arm wrestle with me. If you don't, you're admitting that I am stronger than you."

"Then okay, you can just be stronger than I," Sam replied.

"Look, he's walking away," Wendy said quietly to Elyse.

"Yes, I would say that takes real strength," Elyse said.

"Well, what a yellow-bellied chicken," Darren declared. Just then he saw Gerald coming out of the schoolhouse. "How about an arm wrestling match?" he hollered. "Right here's a picnic table in the shade—a perfect place."

The girls watched as more boys gathered, curious if anyone would arm wrestle Darren.

"Come on, Gerald! Let me show them the strongest one around these parts," Darren bragged.

"Nah, you don't play fair," Gerald replied.

"Come on, don't be a chicken like Sam. A chicken like Sam . . . A chicken like Sam . . ." Darren began chanting.

Then the other boys began their chant, "Show Darren you're a man."

Against all better wisdom, Gerald sat down at the table and Darren joined him. Arms went up and the struggle began. Gerald almost had Darren's arm down when Gerald suddenly cried out, "Stop twisting!"

Sometimes Mirrors Lie

Gerald's arm went down and Darren jumped up. "I'm the strongest!" he bragged. Off he ran toward home, not waiting for the praise of the onlookers. A subdued group of boys broke up and headed home, Gerald cradling his hurting arm against his chest.

"That was a nasty play!" Elyse exclaimed.

"I wish Gerald would have just walked away like Sam did," Wendy said. "He had almost won the game when Darren did that awful twist. Sometimes it takes more strength to walk away than to give in to the challenge."

> A wise man is strong; yea, a man of knowledge increaseth strength.
>
> Proverbs 24:5

"Strength isn't just in the arm or muscle, it is in the character," Elyse said.

"Yes, there is a verse in Proverbs that says, 'A wise man is strong,' and I think Sam showed both wisdom and strength," Wendy added. "But it's so hard sometimes . . . like yesterday."

She lowered her voice. "I saw someone using a calculator for the math test when we were told not to. I wasn't sure what to do."

"What did you decide?" Elyse asked.

"At noon, I told the teacher. Actually, Mr. Hendricks asked me if I had noticed anything wrong during the test, and that made it much easier to tell," Wendy said. "It seems he was watching and was suspicious himself. It was terribly hard. I didn't want to be a tattle-tale, but I didn't want to be dishonest either."

The next day Gerald appeared with his right arm in a sling.

"My ligament is torn and will take a long time to heal," he quietly explained to a crowd of boys gathered around him. "I can't even hold a pencil without pain. Guess I'll have to learn to write with my left hand," he said with a sheepish grin.

Several of the boys spoke up at once. "We're sorry that we egged you on to wrestle, Gerald."

"We all know what Darren does, and he knows what he did too."

"He's not here today for a good reason."

"I was foolish to arm wrestle with him," Gerald admitted. "I knew better—and I hope I can be strong enough to act more wisely from now on."

"Maybe we all learned a lesson," Sam said, glancing at his friend's sling.

"And we all should take a lesson from what you did, Sam," Gerald answered. "Say no and walk away."

Mr. Hendricks realized the boys had been getting carried away with their arm wrestling and boasting. Since the incident with Gerald's arm, they were thinking of strength in a different way. The following day Mr. Hendricks asked his students to write a sentence to answer the question "What is strength?"

A few minutes later he gathered the students' papers and after recess he read some of them aloud.

"Strength is in the heart and not in the muscle."
"Strength is being able to say no when I feel like saying yes."
"When there is no trouble, there is no strength."
"When I ask Him, God will be my strength."

"Strength is being able to walk away when I am called 'yellow.' "

"Strength is being able to say no when I am faced with a challenge I should not accept."

"Strength is being able to say yes when there is a challenge I should face."

"Strength does not fear what others will say about me."

"You students have done very well in defining strength," Mr. Hendricks affirmed. "Now let's prove our strength by choosing wisely in every situation.

"And for the time being, I want the arm wrestling to stop."

Dumb Boys and Prayer

True story

"What's the problem at school?" Mom asked soberly after reading Jerry's weekly report.

"Let me see it. What does it say?" Jerry asked. A guilty frown crossed his face.

"Jerry is not relating well to the younger ones in his class," Jerry read silently.

Jerry tossed the paper onto the table. "Oh, I just can't stand that Rodney! He does the dumbest things. No one likes the Boyers, Mom. I try to stop them from fussing at each other, but that's what they do all the time. Today Rodney and his brother were arguing about who ate the most chicken last evening. They argue over such stupid . . ."

"That's enough," Mom said. "It sounds as though you have

an attitude problem we need to work on. Jerry, it is not your job to control the other children! You are not the schoolroom boss. You need to control yourself—and it would do you good to pray for Rodney."

"Pray for him! I can't do that! What good would that do? Sometimes I pray that I can do what is right and I still get into trouble. Mom, does God answer your prayers?" Jerry asked, nearly in tears.

"Yes, God answers my prayers—but not always in the way I think He should. God wants us to ask Him for help in all things, Jerry, but He doesn't do everything for us. Sometimes we must help answer our own prayers, especially when it comes to an attitude problem. You must do and say things to lessen the problem instead of increasing the irritation," Mom said.

Hear, O my son, and receive my sayings; and the years of thy life shall be many.

Proverbs 4:10

"But Rodney is so dumb! All of us boys think the Boyers have a mental problem, especially Rodney," Jerry exclaimed.

"But I know you, Jerry," Mom replied. "You do 'dumb' little things to get attention too. You must get your eyes off others and watch more what you do yourself. When you pray for Rodney, your attitude toward him will change. If you are interested in improving the situation at school, why don't you ask me to pray with you before you leave for school each morning. Okay?"

"Yes, I can do that," Jerry agreed, "but I really don't see how it's going to help."

Sometimes Mirrors Lie

"You need to believe God will help. And by praying for Rodney, your attitude will change," Mom said again.

The next morning Jerry called Mom to his room and they knelt and prayed together.

"Please, Jesus, help me to get along with Rodney today," Jerry prayed. "Please help me to be good." Then Mom prayed.

After several up and down days, Jerry came home from school and announced, "We boys got together and decided we're going

to try to be real nice to Rodney tomorrow."

"I'm glad to hear that," Dad replied. "Boys from Christian homes, attending a Christian school, shouldn't have trouble getting along. Do you agree?"

"Yes, I guess so."

As Jerry came in the door the next afternoon he exclaimed, "Oh, Mom, school was so much better today!"

But the following day it was a different story.

"School was terrible!" Jerry announced. "Rodney came to school with a patch on his pants, and when someone mentioned it he started making mean remarks about the other boys' pants.

" 'I would stay home before I would wear a patch on my pants,' I told him. Then he said that was a lie—that last year I came to school with patches on my pants all the time. And then we got into a real argument. Verlin said Rodney was right. Mom, I think they are all crazy!

"Mr. Smucker made me stay in at recess and it wasn't even my fault, Mom! It doesn't do any good to pray! I still get into trouble. Rodney's such a trouble-maker! He said I was unkind and that I started the argument, but I didn't."

Mom listened to the outburst, then she said gently, "I'm sorry, Jerry, but your teacher is right. *You* must take responsibility for what you said. That first statement you made to Rodney, 'I would stay home before I would wear a patch on my pants'—was unkind and untrue. Do you forget that you wore patches last year?"

"I didn't wear patches last year!" Jerry declared.

"You did—and what does it matter? Your pants weren't worn

Sometimes Mirrors Lie

out, so I patched the holes you got by sliding during base-ball games. This year you have grown so much we had to buy new pants. They likely will be patched for next year."

"So I really did wear patches last year," Jerry said, rubbing his head. "What a foolish thing to argue about, anyway. So, I suppose I need to apol-ogize to Rodney and the teacher," he added slowly.

> Hear, ye children, the instruction of a father, and attend to know understanding.
> Proverbs 4:1

"Yes, and you need to talk to God about the argument too," Mom said, placing her hand on his shoulder.

o o o o o o o o o o o o o

Jerry came home one day with big news. "Mr. Smucker told Rodney he needs to stay at home for a week and do his schoolwork."

For the next few days Jerry gave glowing reports of a "great day at school." But then one day he came home all gloomy.

"How was school today?" Mom asked.

"Not too good," Jerry mumbled. He went to his room and stayed there until suppertime. Just before supper Mom received a phone call that didn't surprise her.

After supper, Dad, Mom, and Jerry had a talk.

"So you got a spanking at school today?" Dad questioned.

"How'd you find out?" Jerry asked, keeping his eyes on his shoes.

"Mr. Smucker called. You tell us about it," Dad urged.

"Well, Verlin and I got in a fight!" Jerry said, still looking at his shoes as though he was afraid they would leave his feet.

"Oh?" Dad said.

"Well, not really a fight—I just pushed Verlin over. But Dad, he laughed because I got 75% on math. It was his fault! That's not the way for a supposed-to-be friend to act!"

"Rodney wasn't at school, so you can't blame your problem on him. But now it's Verlin's fault. Someone else is always getting you into trouble," Mom said with reproach in her voice. "What about your personal responsibility, son?"

"Oh, Mom, I suppose you're right. It's probably often my own fault when I get into trouble," Jerry said. "And now I know how it feels to be laughed at. I guess if we boys still have trouble even when Rodney isn't in school, it shows that our problems are not all his fault."

"I am glad you see that now," Dad said. "I think you may have come to the beginning of the end of some of your troubles. With God's help, you boys can be loving and kind to each other."

"I hope Rodney comes back to school soon," Jerry said. "It must not be much fun to be at home alone when the rest of us are in school. He really isn't any more of a trouble-maker than the rest of us boys are sometimes."

"So praying for him has helped?" Mom asked.

"Yes, I think it has," Jerry replied after a bit. "And I want to be nice to Rodney when he comes back to school."

The Knitting Machine

True story

"Mother, may I use the knitting machine?" Matt called from the sewing room. "Please, I want to knit a rug."

"I think you would do better at braiding a rug," Mother replied, "and a braided rug would last much longer."

"I don't want to braid—that's a girl's job," Matt said in exasperation. "I want to run a machine— the knitting machine!"

When she heard some noise a little later, Mother hurried to the sewing room to see what Matt might be doing. He had been begging to use the machine, but she wasn't sure he would follow instructions. "Please don't play with the machine," Mother said.

"But Mom, I need to see how it works," Matt explained. "Please let me knit."

"We've been over this before," Mother began.

"Yes, I know! You think I'll start and not finish. You think I'll go too fast and drop stitches. You think I'll get angry when things don't go right. You think . . ."

"Well, it seems you're aware of the possible problems. Do you think you will be able to bypass them all?"

"Yes, yes, just let me make a rug," Matt begged.

Mother raised her eyebrows. "How about making something smaller—like a spread for your dresser?"

"Oh—well, I guess that's better than nothing," Matt conceded, seeing his mother's doubtful expression.

"Okay, I'll do a spread first—and then prove that I can do a rug too," Matt said with saucy grin.

Mother got the machine all set with the yarn and helped Matt with the first several rows. As soon as Mother left the room Matt remarked, "This is great. These rows are so short it will be finished in no time."

Back and forth he moved the carriage. Back and forth he added row after row. He began going faster and then even faster.

"Slow down," Mother warned when she heard the machine speeding up.

Suddenly the carriage stopped. Matt groaned and called out, "Come, Mother! I need help. I dropped some stitches."

"You were going much too fast," Mother said. She worked at picking up the dropped stitches as she explained, "Every time you drop a stitch it will leave a scar on your spread."

"Well, you picked up the stitch. Why should it leave a scar?" Matt asked.

"Every time you drop a stitch and keep on knitting, that

dropped stitch causes missing stitches in the next rows." Then she left him on his own again.

"Oh, well, this spread will have some scars," Matt said.

Again he began moving the carriage back and forth, slowly at first and then faster and faster. "Mother, I need help," he called again.

After calling for help several times, Matt's patience began to run out. *When will I ever get done?* he wondered. "Mom, come help me finish," he begged. "I'm so tired of this crazy machine. It doesn't work right. My spread is all scarred."

Mother came but she did not help. "No, Matt. This is your project and you must finish it. If you would follow my instructions and go more slowly you would not drop so many stitches."

"But Mother, I want to get finished!"

"Slow down and you *will* get finished," Mother advised.

"No, I must go faster if I am to get done," Matt said stubbornly.

"Slow down and you will get finished," Mother said again. " 'A job well begun is half done.' "

"This job isn't even well begun. This is so scarred it is not fit for my dresser!" Matt cried at last. "I never want to knit again! I'm quitting. I'm going outside to ride my bike. I'm tired of this old knitting machine. It just doesn't work right." And out the door Matt went.

> Trust in the Lord with all thine heart; and lean not unto thine own understanding. In all thy ways acknowledge him, and he shall direct thy paths. Proverbs 3:5, 6

"Hmmm," Mother sighed. It was just as she had feared it would be. The job was too tedious for Matt.

After lunch Mother said, "Matt, I want you to try again on the project you started with the knitting machine. I want you to learn to finish what you start."

"I don't want to knit. That machine doesn't work right," Matt complained.

"It will work right if you slow down," Mother said patiently.

Matt trudged to the sewing room. He sat down at the machine and slowly began again. He didn't want to be a quitter, but he sure didn't feel like finishing either. Faster and faster he moved the carriage.

Again Mother called out, "Slow down, Matt. You'll drop stitches . . ."

"I already did and this spread looks horrid!" Matt wailed.

Mother came to the sewing room and sat down beside Matt. "Look at me, Matt," she said.

When his eyes met hers, she went on. "You know, when you don't listen to what I say, you are making a scar on your heart. Every time you disobey, you make a scar. Every time you insist on your own way, you make a scar. And every time you get angry, it adds another scar."

"Oh, Mother, then my heart is full of scars—like this spread?" Matt questioned.

"Yes, Matt. But there is good news . . . Jesus can forgive those scars and take them away if you ask Him to. Tell Him you are sorry and want to do better. He can help you to stop going your own way and learn to obey Him and listen to your parents."

Matt sighed. "Why is it so hard to do what you tell me to do, Mother?"

"Well, Matt, you are a very strong-willed young man. You know what you want to do and you do it, even when you are told not to. That willfulness is wrong, but your determination can be a great help in life—if you will learn to stop and ask what God wants you to do and follow instructions. That's what the verse in Proverbs means that says, 'In all thy ways acknowledge him, and he shall direct thy paths.' God is always ready and waiting to help us make the right choices. We just have to remember to consider His will and follow His way."

"That's going to be a hard one for me to remember, but I will try!" Matt promised.

Mr. Ornery

The back door slammed behind Brad as he came into the kitchen. "That Mr. Ornery, I wish he would move."

His mother frowned. "Please, Brad, call him Mr. Horner. No more Mr. Ornery." She glanced out the window at the house next door. "What has he done now that has you so upset?"

Brad shook his head. He chose an apple from the bowl on the table and took a huge bite. He chewed for a bit before he answered. "He yelled and told me to stay out of his yard. And all I was doing was getting my Frisbee after it flew onto his lawn. If I hadn't gone after it, he would have been mad because it was there. It's a no-win situation with him."

Mom nodded. "I know he seems to be hard to get along with, Brad, but I really wish you'd try. Dad talked with him one day when the mailman mistakenly gave us some of his mail. Mr. Horner was polite and thanked him for bringing it over. We should try to be friends."

He that followeth after righteousness and mercy findeth life, righteousness, and honour. Proverbs 21:21

Mom thought a bit, then added, "The next time I bake muffins, I'll make some extra and take them over to him. People who live alone often don't bake things for themselves."

Brad nodded and climbed the stairs to his room. He flung the Frisbee into a corner and flopped down on the bed. The Bible verse his mother had embroidered and hung on his wall caught his eye. "Do unto others as you would have them do unto you." It was a rule he tried to live by. Mom and Dad did a better job of it than he did, though. Most of the time it wasn't hard to do, but Mr. Ornery—oops, Mr. Horner—sure made it difficult.

Brad lay on his bed thinking. He had tried many times to be friends with Mr. Horner. He waved to him if he saw him out in his yard. Once he had picked up Mr. Horner's newspaper and given it to him when the carrier dropped it on the road. Mr. Horner had complained because it was dirty and acted as if it were Brad's fault. Brad had shoveled snow off the sidewalk in front of his neighbor's house after he finished his own family's sidewalk—but Mr. Horner hadn't even bothered to say thank you.

Brad remembered the day soon after his family had moved in next door to Mr. Horner. He had been outside playing with

Sometimes Mirrors Lie

Emmy, his beagle. The dog had run over to Mr. Horner's yard and was sniffing around. Suddenly the door opened and Mr. Horner had yelled out, "Keep that dog off my grass. If she messes in my yard you'll have to come clean it up! I don't want any stinkin' dog in my yard." Brad's heart still pounded hard when he thought of the incident. He had been so angry and disappointed. He had been hoping for a nice neighbor boy to play with. But instead of a friend, he had a grouchy old man next door.

Last winter Brad and his friend Tim had been in the back yard. They were laughing and scooping up snowballs and throwing them at each other when suddenly Mr. Horner opened his door and yelled, "You boys stop that before you break a window!"

Brad could feel his face turning hot and red at the memory. Now today with the Frisbee marked the third time. *Three times and you're out,* Brad thought. *I've tried to be nice to him but he hasn't been nice to me. We've lived here for months and not once has he even smiled or said "Hi" to me. He doesn't want to be friends and I don't want to be friends with him, either.*

But Brad's thoughts didn't make his heart feel any better. Why did his memories cause him to feel so upset and angry? *I guess I have never forgiven Mr. Horner and am holding grudges,* he thought. *What's that quote Mom always tells me? Oh, "Anger is a poison that will kill you before it kills your enemy." I guess that means I'm hurting myself more than I'm hurting Mr. Horner. I need a huge dose of forgiveness, as Mom would say.*

The next morning Brad was taking out the garbage when he heard someone calling, "Help! Help me, somebody!" It seemed to be coming from Mr. Horner's yard.

Brad ran around the corner of the garage and saw Mr. Horner up in his maple tree. He was holding onto a limb, but his legs were dangling, and he was too high up to drop to the ground. The ladder below him had tipped over.

> A fool's wrath is presently known: but a prudent man covereth shame. Proverbs 12:16

"Hold on a minute, Mr. Horner, I'll help you," Brad called out. He hurried over and picked up the ladder. It took a minute or two to get it between the branches so Mr. Horner could reach it.

Mr. Horner eased his feet onto the highest rung and began climbing down. When he reached the ground, he took a handkerchief from his back pocket and wiped his forehead. Then he sat down on a nearby stump and exhaled a long breath. "Thank you for coming over, boy," he said. "I don't think I could have held on much longer. I climbed into the tree and was trying to saw off a dead limb when the one I was standing on broke and knocked over the ladder."

"I'm glad I could help," Brad said.

Mr. Horner sighed. "I guess I couldn't blame you if you hadn't come to my rescue. I haven't treated you very well."

Brad didn't answer. What could he say? Mr. Horner was simply stating the truth.

"I want you to know I'm sorry. I should have been a better neighbor." He paused. "I once had some boys tear up my yard and another time they stole watermelons out of my garden. . . .

It made me sour about any youngsters coming onto my property. But I guess you're not all the same, are you?"

"No, sir," Brad said.

"You had every right to ignore me, to treat me the way I treated you. You could have left me hanging in that tree. Why didn't you?" Mr. Horner asked.

"In our family we try to follow the golden rule," Brad said. "My folks tell me, 'Do unto others as you would have them do unto you.' If I were up a tree and couldn't get down, I'd want someone to help me."

Mr. Horner nodded. "I learned the golden rule when I was young too. Guess I kind of forgot it. I'm glad you reminded me." He smiled. "From now on, I'll try to follow it too, okay?"

Brad grinned. "Shall I put the ladder away for you?"

"Sure, thanks." Mr. Horner picked up the saw and the two neighbors walked side-by-side toward the garage. Brad placed the ladder on the wall hooks Mr. Horner indicated, then turned to go.

"Bye, Mr. Orn—I mean, Mr. Horner."

Then he added to himself, *I'll never call you Mr. Ornery again.*

—Marie Latta

When Stubbornness Explodes

Based on a true incident

"Tyler, the yard needs to be mowed today," Mom said after breakfast. "It would be best to do it before it gets too hot."

"Well, Todd and I planned to go fishing," Tyler announced.

Mom frowned. "Tyler, you must not make plans before you ask permission. I'm sorry, but you may not go fishing. You know we are having company tomorrow and the lawn and trash must be done today. Call Todd and tell him it doesn't suit."

Tyler slammed the door behind him as he left the kitchen. He would call Todd later. He went to the shed and yanked the mower out into the yard. *How in the world can a fellow be happy when his mother is constantly telling him what to do?* he wondered.

As Tyler pushed the mower back and forth, his conscience

began speaking to him. *Stop resenting instruction! Your parents really do know what is best. Open your eyes to what needs to be done and offer to do it before you are told.*

> The way of a fool is right in his own eyes: but he that hearkeneth unto counsel is wise.
> Proverbs 12:15

But another voice in his head argued, *I want to go fishing. It's such a pain having someone always telling me what to do next. I really would like to make some of my own decisions.* He had been through this mental battle before. By the time the lawn was mowed, he was exhausted and discouraged.

He called Todd and canceled the plans, then sat on the front porch with his book.

"Did you forget about the trash, Tyler?" Mom reminded. "Please check that there are no spray cans in the trash. Spray cans are very dangerous in fire. They can explode."

"Yes, yes, Mom," Tyler groaned. Then he mumbled, "A boy would think he doesn't know anything with a mother always telling him what to do and not to do. I think it would be neat to see a spray can explode."

Tyler grabbed the trash and tromped to the burn pile. "I get so sick and tired of being told what to do," he muttered. "I know about spray cans. I know all about burning trash! How many times have I done this job!"

He dumped the trash onto the pile and out rolled a spray can. "Well, let's see what will happen," he said. Deliberately, he held a match to the pile—without removing the spray can.

Then he stepped back a few feet and watched for a few minutes. The flames spread through the paper trash and grew hotter.

"See, just what I knew would happen—nothing!"

He bent to get a stick to poke the can. And then it happened.

Boom! A scream of terror filled the air, so loud that Mom heard it from inside the house.

Mom came running across the back yard. She pushed Tyler

down onto the grass and tried to roll him to put out the fire on his burning shirt. That is the last he remembered for a while.

In the emergency room, Tyler was given strong pain medication and cleaned up as much as possible; then he was admitted to the hospital in a semi-conscious state. His face and torso had been badly burned. When the doctor arrived, his mother was sitting by his side, in tears.

"Mrs. Shaffer, I am very sorry about your son's accident. I am Doctor Olsen."

Tyler's mother lifted her teary face and shook the doctor's outstretched hand.

"Tyler's burn is very serious, Mrs. Shaffer," the doctor said. "It will take a long time to heal and there will be much scar damage. The important thing right now is to keep him from getting an infection. First he will need to have surgery to remove the burned skin; then we will take skin from his upper leg for the graft. We do have a skin graft bank as a resource, but I'm sure he will have enough good skin of his own for the grafts."

"Will he . . . will he always look deformed?" Mrs. Shaffer asked.

"Skin grafting can do only so much. His burn is very deep," the doctor replied.

The company, the meal, the house . . . all was forgotten as Mrs. Shaffer kept vigilance by Tyler's bed. Mr. Shaffer came in the evening after work. After one look at his son, he hurried out of the room. After some time he returned and took his wife into his arms and they cried together.

At last he asked, "What are we going to do?"

Sometimes Mirrors Lie

"There is nothing we can do. He is in God's hands and God will have to take care of him." Then Mrs. Shaffer explained what the doctor had told her. It was decided that she would stay at the hospital and her husband would bring her what she needed each evening after work. When her husband was ready to leave, she asked, "Will you call the church hotline and ask for prayer for Tyler? And please call my mother and your mother and tell them what is going on."

A cot was set up in Tyler's room for his mother. Most of the time he was so sedated that he didn't know she was there, but he often moaned in his restless sleep.

"Today we plan to do surgery to remove the burned skin," the doctor said one morning. "Tyler will be out for six or seven hours. Mrs. Shaffer, why don't you go home and do something relaxing."

Mrs. Shaffer was glad to get out of the hospital for several hours. But find something relaxing? Would she ever feel relaxed again? It looked like a terribly long and difficult road ahead of them. How would Tyler accept his deformed face? How she prayed the skin graft would take care of it.

A few mornings later, Tyler opened his eyes and looked around the room for the first time. "Where am I?" he asked in a hoarse voice.

His mother was at his side. "You are in the hospital, Tyler."

"Why am I here?" he asked. "Why does it hurt when I talk?" He tried to

> He that trusteth in his own heart is a fool: but whoso walketh wisely, he shall be delivered.
> Proverbs 28:26

reach up to his face but found his hands were tied down. "Why are my hands tied?" he asked in exasperation.

"You burned yourself, and the doctor doesn't want you to touch your face," his mother answered. "Do you remember?"

"Oh, that spray can!" Tyler exclaimed. "I'm sorry, Mom! I should have listened to you."

Mrs. Shaffer sent up a quick prayer. *Thank you, God. His mind is all right. I was afraid he wouldn't be in his right mind—I guess because he doesn't look like Tyler.*

The doctor came in and saw Tyler was awake. "How are you doing, buddy?"

Without answering the doctor's question, Tyler asked, "Do you have a mirror? I want to see myself. My face feels funny."

"No mirror yet," the doctor replied. "Your face is all bandaged. How do you like that sunshine coming in the window?"

"I like the sunshine but I would rather be outside in it. When can I get up and go out?"

"I think you can get up and walk around tomorrow, but it will be a little while before you can go out," the doctor replied.

The next morning Tyler awoke excited. "Today I can walk, Mom. Will you walk with me?"

"Yes, of course I will walk with you, but let's have breakfast first," she said with a smile.

A nurse came in after breakfast and helped Tyler slowly get out of bed. "Now move slowly and carefully. You haven't walked for several days and you may feel dizzy."

Tyler stood on his feet, but his legs felt shaky. "My head feels like it's going in circles."

"That is because you have been lying down so long," the nurse explained. "That is why you must walk slowly."

Mom held Tyler's arm and they walked slowly down the hall, then turned around and walked back to his room.

"Can I sit down on this chair instead of going back to bed?" Tyler asked. "I do feel tired."

After he was settled in the chair he asked the question that was bothering him. "Mama, why did some of the nurses crunch up their faces when I walked past?"

"Well, Tyler, I do not know for sure," Mom said, trying to think of what she should tell her son. "A burn on the face changes the way a person looks."

"I must look terrible!" Tyler exclaimed. "Most of those nurses didn't even smile at me."

"Tyler, you do not look the same as you did before the fire," Mom tried to explain. "People will react in many different ways when they look at your face.

"But I want you to always remember: it isn't your face that tells people what kind of boy you are—it is your character. If you are kind, honest, loving, and caring about others, they will see you as a lovely person on the inside."

Tyler thought about that for a while.

"But . . . Mom," he faltered, "if I look . . . ugly . . . will the children still play with me? Will they want me to be their friend at school? How can I show them what I am on the inside when they only look at my face on the outside?"

"It may take some time, and you will likely feel hurt often until you prove to them that you are good and loving on the inside. It's not going to be easy, Tyler. This trial could make you strong, compassionate, and beautiful—or it could make you bitter, angry, and hateful. The decision is up to you. With God's help, son, you can make the right choices."

When a Milker Met a Tooth

True story

Andy placed his hand on the latch to the chicken pen. He glanced around, but no one else was in sight. He opened the chickens' gate. As soon as they spotted the opening, they ran like a bunch of children just let out of school. "Just see how they love that grass!" Andy exclaimed. "And look how they snap up the bugs."

He turned and walked toward the barn. But his delight in letting the chickens run began to fade fast as he saw them headed into Mother's flower borders around the house. *Oh well, I don't have time to shoo them back before chores and school.*

At the breakfast table, Mother happened to glance out the window. "Oh, no! Who let the chickens out? They are in my flowers!"

She looked around the table but no one answered. Finally Andy's older brother Albert spoke up. "It probably was Andy."

Andy felt his neck muscles tighten. "Why is it always 'probably Andy'?" he demanded. "Why do you always think I'm the one who does all the wrong things?"

"Was it you, son?" Father asked, looking directly at Andy.

"Yes, I let them out. They love the grass and the bugs. It's a shame to pen them up on a sunny, beautiful day," Andy exclaimed.

"It is more of a shame that they mess up the flower beds which your mother has worked so hard at," Father replied.

"I will put them in when I get home from school," Andy said, rising from the table.

"No," Father insisted, "you will put them back in the pen right now."

"But I will be late for school."

"Yes, you will be late, but maybe that will help you remember my instructions. You know the chickens are to be kept in their pen."

Andy sighed and headed outside. He grabbed the broom and hurried toward the chickens, shooing them from the flower beds. The more he waved the broom the more they cackled and ran in all directions.

"I'll never get to school at this rate," Andy complained as Father came out of the house.

"You must direct them more calmly," Father said. "Why don't you get a little bucket of feed and see if they will follow you to the chicken coop that way."

"Hummph. *Someday* I'll be my own boss and do things *my* way," Andy said under his breath.

"And hopefully on that *someday* you will be more mature and behave more wisely," Father said. "Just remember we are never our own boss. Either God or Satan will be in control." He placed an encouraging hand on Andy's shoulder before disappearing around the shed.

Maybe someday they all will understand me better and trust me more, Andy thought dejectedly. Life seemed to be even more difficult now that he was a teenager.

Andy tried his own way a little longer, waving the broom and hollering at the chickens. It just wasn't working, so he gave up. With reluctant feet, he headed for the feed bin. He filled a small bucket and did as his father had suggested. What a wonder. It worked. *I guess Father knew what he was talking about,* he admitted.

That afternoon Andy found himself with some homework because of his late arrival at school. Then it was time for chores. Where had the afternoon gone?

In the barn, one of the heifers had just given birth to her first calf the night before. Any good farmer knows that a fresh heifer can be very unpredictable.

Albert called out to Andy as soon as he entered the barn, "Andy, don't put the milker on that fresh cow. Do you hear?"

"Yeah, I hear," Andy answered. *I put the milker on her this morning and it went okay,* he reasoned. What a pain to always have an older brother bossing! He grabbed the milker and headed for the fresh cow.

Sometimes Mirrors Lie

Albert came around the corner. "I said, 'Don't put the milker on that cow!' "

"I can put the milker on that cow if I want to."

Albert warned again, "Better not!"

But Andy did not stop. The cow was a small Jersey and had scooted to the far side of the stanchion. Andy swung the milker in carelessly. He would prove that he could handle this cow. But when Andy swung the milker under the little Jersey, it hit her foot. The cow's foot shot out in protest. Faster than he could comprehend, the milker flew up and hit him right in the mouth, landing soundly on a tooth.

"Oh, ouch!" Andy exclaimed. He placed a trembling hand on his mouth—and found blood. He would have a fat lip tomorrow. Then he felt his tooth. Oh, no, over half of it was missing—and it hurt fiercely! He began looking for the broken piece of his tooth.

He that refuseth instruction despiseth his own soul: but he that heareth reproof getteth understanding.

Proverbs 15:32

"Didn't I tell you not to put the milker on that cow?" Albert said with exasperation.

Andy just glared at him and headed for the house. He was not able to help finish the chores that evening. As he sat in a chair moaning and holding ice over his lip and tooth, he did some serious thinking. A fresh heifer did not like her udder to be touched, nor did she like a milker banging her foot! He knew that! He should have been more careful. But that heifer had stood for him this morning—and he had needed to prove to his brother that she would be okay with the milker tonight.

Really?

Andy rethought his last notion. The truth was—he didn't really *need* to prove anything to his brother. What he needed to do was to listen to others who had experience. Perhaps life would be easier if he would follow instructions.

The following morning, Andy and his mother went to the dentist to get a crown put onto his tooth. That tooth would remind him the rest of his life that to insist on his own way was folly. It is wiser to take instructions from others.

—James Beachy

The Bridge of Forgiveness

True story

○ ○ ○ ○ ○ ○ ○ ○ ○ ○ ○ ○ ○ ○

How can we forgive when someone has hurt us so terribly that it feels like our hearts are broken into pieces? How can we remove from our memories the most terrible happening we have ever witnessed?

Ashley still asks herself these questions at times. Though the passage of time and efforts to forgive have lessened the hurt of her loss, Ashley can still vividly recall the incident.

○ ○ ○ ○ ○ ○ ○ ○ ○ ○ ○ ○ ○ ○

The Mississippi sun seemed to be begging the girls to head for the creek that beautiful, warm day. Ashley and her sister Sharla loved to swim, and it was even more fun with their friends. Today the neighbor girls had brought along a friend from the city.

"Kelli, do you know how to swim?" thirteen-year-old Ashley asked as the girls headed for the creek.

"Of course I can swim!" Kelli replied, "I can swim as good as any of you. We have pools in the city!"

The cool water beckoned the girls and before long they were all splashing merrily. Twelve-year-old Sharla was soon out in the deeper water in the middle of the creek. Not to be outdone, but without fathoming the danger, Kelli followed her.

Suddenly Kelli realized she was in deep water. In panic, she grabbed Sharla.

"Let go of me!" Sharla yelled. "Paddle your feet and arms and let me go!"

Sharla struggled to get loose, but as Kelli went underwater, she pulled Sharla along down. Her feet rested on Sharla as she frantically tried to keep her head above water. Frightened screams filled the sultry air.

"Kelli, get off my sister!" Ashley shrieked as she came as close as she could without going under herself. "Swim!"

"I can't! I can't swim!" Kelli cried out in desperation.

"Kelli! You have to get off Sharla!" the neighbor girls cried. "She can't breathe!" But all their words were to no avail as Kelli simply stared in wide-eyed terror.

Frantically the girls looked around for a board or something. "Here, grab this air mattress! It will help you float." Quickly Kelli grabbed the air mattress and came toward shore.

The girls watched the spot where they had last seen Sharla. But she did not come to the surface. She was under the water,

Sometimes Mirrors Lie

and none of the girls were good at diving. The girls ran for help and then hurried back to the creek, hoping that somehow Sharla would be there on the shore. She wasn't.

The rescue squad arrived a few minutes later. They soon found Sharla's body and tried to revive her. But her life was gone. The angels had already carried her to the place of peace and rest.

"Oh, why did we ever bring Kelli over here?" the neighbor girls cried. "We wondered if she really knew how to swim. Where is she anyway?"

"I—I saw her run back to your house," Ashley replied between sobs.

By this time the family and the neighbors had arrived and were gathering around Sharla's lifeless body.

"That child ought to be sent to a detention home for a year," one neighbor said. "Maybe that would teach her something."

"You should sue her family!" others said angrily.

Sharla's mother spoke up quietly. "I think the child just panicked and didn't know what to do. She didn't do it on purpose."

Several of the girls spoke at once, "We told Kelli to get off Sharla! We told her to swim, but she just stood there on top of Sharla."

Someone spoke from the center of the crowd, "Maybe we each need to put ourselves in Kelli's place. What would we have done if we couldn't swim? What if we had panicked in deep water? How would we feel if we had caused such a horrible accident?"

The crowd grew quiet as they pondered those words. *What would I have done? How would I feel now?*

Slowly the neighbors returned to their homes, and Sharla's

family watched as the coroner placed her body in the hearse and drove away to the funeral home.

Anger, frustration, and revenge are not the ways of God or His children. God's way is forgiveness and doing to others as we would have them do to us. Sharla's family knew that.

But . . . forgive? Was God really expecting them to forgive this simple city girl for causing their daughter and sister to drown? The family discussed this a number of times in the weeks following the funeral, often through flowing tears. Forgive? How?

> Hatred stirreth up strifes: but love covereth all sins. Proverbs 10:12

"Yes, God is asking us to forgive," said Sandy, Ashley's older sister. "Forgiveness isn't easy, but with God's grace it is possible. Forgiveness is something that needs to be worked on—it doesn't come automatically. First we must *want* to forgive. Then we must ask God to *help* us forgive. Forgiveness means thinking more of the offending person than of my own personal hurt."

"When I make the decision to forgive, I have to pray and ask God for strength to forgive and love the person who has wronged me—wronged our whole family," Mother added. "Forgiveness does not excuse the other person's wrong, but if we refuse to forgive, we become a slave to our grudge and wallow in bitterness. But when we forgive, we free ourselves so we can move on with our lives."

"Well, what do I do when the terrible scene at the creek comes to my mind and I feel bitter and angry?" Ashley asked.

Sometimes Mirrors Lie

"Those memories will likely come back to each of us time and again, especially to you, Ashley, and then we must go to God again and ask for a forgiving and loving attitude," Mother replied. "Whether the hurt comes from losing a loved one, having a false rumor spread about you, or an unintentional slight of a friend, just remember God is able to help if we are willing to let it go.

"But I still think I will always hate that girl," their brother Howard protested. "She made my sister drown!"

No one spoke for a minute. Howard was not alone. They all struggled with similar feelings.

Finally Sandy replied, "I try to remember that if I hold on to anger and frustration, I break the bridge that spans the gap between me and God. I need forgiveness too sometimes—many times. God won't forgive me if I do not forgive another."

"Jesus prayed that His enemies would be forgiven for their unjust, cruel treatment," Dad said. "He said, 'Father, forgive them; for they know not what they do.' Jesus still carries the scars of their evil deeds, but those scars are healed. They are not sore, festering gashes."

"We may need to keep reminding each other of this so that we can continue to heal," Mother said tearfully.

"This scar will always mark our family, but let it be a healed scar, not a festering one," Dad encouraged. "That is the beauty of forgiveness!"

—Carol Bechtel

The Bridge of Forgiveness

The Tractor and Travis

True story

Travis was almost holding his breath that Monday morning as the Randall family gathered around the breakfast table. He hoped Mom wouldn't ask him to help hang out the wash. Usually his sister did that job, but today she was working at the neighbors. He was hoping he would get to drive the tractor sometime today.

"Well Travis, what did you learn in Sunday school yesterday morning?" Dad asked. That was his usual Monday morning question.

"We talked about the fool eating the fruit of his own way," Travis said, taking a drink of orange juice.

"That sounds interesting," Mom said. "Can you give us an example?"

"Well, the verse says something about not accepting counsel

and despising reproof and being filled with their own devices. The teacher did explain it some. He said it means people who don't follow instructions and go their own way instead," Travis finished.

Then he looked around at the knowing grins. "What are you all smiling about?"

"That sounds just like my little brother," Eric laughed.

"Don't call me your little brother! Just because I'm short doesn't mean I'm little, and I listen to instruction—most of the time."

"Who can tell us what eating the 'fruit of their own way' means?" Dad asked.

"Could it be like the time Travis kept sneaking cookies from the freezer and ate too many and got sick?" Nicole asked. Everyone was smiling, even Travis.

"Yes, cookies were the fruit of my sneaking and the cause of my sickness," Travis admitted. "But how about an example from somebody else besides me?"

"Well, I remember once when I was younger I dressed up the kitty and took it for a real fast ride in my baby buggy," Nicole said. "The kitty got sick and made a mess all over her clothes and the buggy and blanket. Mom made me rinse everything at the outside faucet before she would wash the things in her washer. I guess going too fast made the kitten get sick—and the fruit of my behavior was the mess I had to clean up." Nicole wrinkled her nose and laughed at the memory.

"And how about an example from the big brother?" Dad suggested.

"Sure," Eric said. "I remember that rainy April morning when

Mom told me to wear my boots to school. But I didn't want to be encumbered with heavy boots while we were playing Dare Base, so I just wore my tennis shoes. There were mud puddles all over and my feet got very wet. By the time I came home I was shivering with cold. I didn't eat much supper and went to bed early. During the night I had fever and in the morning I couldn't go to school because I was sick."

> They would none of my counsel: they despised all my reproof. Therefore shall they eat of the fruit of their own way, and be filled with their own devices.
> Proverbs 1:30, 31

"Well, I'm sure we have all acted foolishly and had to reap the results," Dad said. "Such lessons should teach us to choose carefully what we will say or do, or how we will act.

"Well, let's get going. It's time to start the day."

As the men stepped outside, Dad told Travis, "You may drive the tractor to the back of the field and see if Betsy had her calf."

Travis felt like clapping his hands and jumping into the air, but he was too big for that. He was just learning to drive the Ford tractor. He felt big and powerful as he climbed up on the tractor seat.

"Now, Travis," Dad had said, "I want you to remember: You are just learning how to handle this tractor and I want you to drive it no faster than third gear. This machine has more power than you know how to control right now."

"Yes, Dad, I know. I'm small and you think I'm weak," Travis groaned.

"Be a wise son and listen up!" Dad said with a grin.

"Yes, of course," Travis replied.

Travis started the tractor and headed for the back field. How big and important he felt! He would try hard to follow his father's instructions.

◦ ◦ ◦ ◦ ◦ ◦ ◦ ◦ ◦ ◦ ◦ ◦ ◦ ◦

Several weeks later Travis was in the yard when Eric drove the tractor out of the barn. He had just finished scraping the alleys between the free stalls. Travis ran up alongside the tractor. "Hey, Eric, let me drive up to the shop. Please-e-se, let me drive it," Travis begged.

Grudgingly Eric replied, "Okay, you can drive, but I will beat you up to the shop."

The challenge was on! Travis jumped onto the tractor seat. He pushed in the clutch and shoved the gear shift into third gear—but the tractor was simply not going fast enough to suit him. *I'll never beat Eric at this speed! Dad isn't home anyway and he will never know if I use a higher gear.*

Travis put the tractor into fourth gear—still not fast enough. Then he put it into fifth. Away Travis flew with the tractor—at least he *felt* like he was flying. He would have to drive around the milk house and up the hill to the shop. Eric could take a shortcut between the buildings and get up to the shop faster than he could.

The tractor whizzed around the milk house and around the corner, where a rut washed out across the lane. That little Ford tractor did not have power steering and the front wheel caught—right in that rut. Desperately Travis tried to steer the tractor out of the rut but he could not. He looked up just in time to see the block wall of the milk house looming in front of him.

Crash! The tractor, with Travis driving, hit the corner of the milk house. The compressor for the milk tank was right inside

the corner and that is the only thing that kept the tractor from going on into the milk house.

In panic, Travis jumped up and down on the immobile tractor, its motor still roaring. "Help! Help! I can't stop the tractor!" he screamed.

"Turn it off!" Eric hollered. "Turn it off!"

"I can't!" Travis yelled back, still jumping up and down. He couldn't think what to do.

Eric came running. He reached up and turned the key to the off position—and that was the end of the race.

Needless to say, Dad found out that Travis had driven the tractor in a higher gear than he was supposed to. All evening Travis felt weak and shaky. He felt foolish for his behavior and sorry for his disobedience. Now Dad would have to fix both the tractor and the milk house wall.

When Travis's friends at school learned of the accident, they laughed at him for running into the milk house. Travis was afraid he would "eat of the fruit" of his foolishness for a long time. And for an even longer time, the bright new blocks glared at Travis from the corner of the milk house. They reminded him that it never pays to disobey instructions.

—James Beachy

Silly as a Goose

Based on fact

Kevin grinned as he stepped into the hall for last break. The school day was almost over, and he was feeling pretty good—he had managed to stay out of trouble today.

Then he heard Vince call his name. "Hey, Kevin, come here. Look at this cute little green frog. I dare you to put it into Marla's lunchbox."

"No, that wouldn't be nice," Kevin replied.

"Oh, Kevin, don't be such a softy. You know Marla loves frogs," Vince said with a grin.

Wayne suddenly appeared with another frog. "I'll put this frog in Sherry's lunchbox if you put that one in Marla's lunchbox," he said with a wink.

"Sure. Come on—let's go into the schoolhouse before the

bell rings," Vince said, carrying the frog in one hand and grabbing Kevin's arm with the other.

The boys found the lunchboxes, but Kevin hesitated. Vince put the frog into Kevin's hand and said, "Now don't be a chicken. Quick! Put it in Marla's box."

Kevin dropped it in and closed the lid of the lunchbox. "Okay, Wayne, you put your frog in Sherry's box."

"No way! I don't want to get into trouble."

"But you want *me* to get into trouble!" Kevin exclaimed angrily.

Suddenly the bell rang and the boys hurried to their seats.

The last hour and a half of the school day dragged. Kevin was so angry he could not think straight. The boys had tricked him again. They never did what they said they were going to do, and he was the only one who always got into trouble.

> He that trusteth in his own heart is a fool: but whoso walketh wisely, he shall be delivered.
>
> Proverbs 28:26

Finally the last bell rang. Marla picked up her lunch box and opened it to put something inside. Suddenly she screamed. The teacher hurried to her side. "What's wrong, Marla?"

In a shaky voice Marla replied, "Oh, just a little frog in my lunch pail."

Miss Carla rang her desk bell and told the students to return to their seats. Then she said quietly, "We are not leaving here until we find out who put the frog in Marla's lunch pail."

Soon Wayne's hand was waving in the air. "I saw Kevin do it," he said with a smirk.

Sometimes Mirrors Lie

Miss Carla looked at Kevin with questioning eyes. "Yes, I did it with Wayne's help," he admitted.

The teacher asked Wayne and Kevin to stay while the rest of the students were dismissed.

When Kevin was late coming out to the waiting car, Mother knew something had happened. He slammed the car door and they drove toward home in silence.

Mother was waiting for Kevin to calm down so he could tell her about it. Finally the story poured from the depths of his hurting heart. As she put her arms around him comfortingly she pondered her response. *Why is Kevin always getting into trouble? Does he need knowledge or does he need courage?*

"Kevin," she said, "do you remember those three geese we saw again this morning?"

Yes, Kevin remembered well. They had been in the middle of the road—and instead of being afraid when his mother had tooted the horn, they had attacked the car tires, hissing and honking with necks outstretched, snapping at the tires. And it was not the first time they had done it.

"You silly geese!" Kevin often exclaimed. "Do you suppose you can bite a hole in the tire?"

"You'd think they'd be afraid of those huge black tires rolling toward them," Kevin's mother said. "Do you think those geese have courage or do they act foolishly?"

"They act foolishly," Kevin replied after a brief pause.

"Maybe that's why we have that saying, 'As silly as a goose,'" Mother continued. "A goose probably does silly things because it doesn't know better, but a fool does foolish things because he doesn't have the courage to do right."

Kevin looked up at Mother. "Sometimes I act like a silly goose," he admitted. "Just like today when I put that frog in Marla's lunch pail. I don't know why I let those boys trick me like that. I hope I can do a better job of staying out of trouble from now on."

Sometimes Mirrors Lie

A few days later when Kevin's mother picked him up after school, Kevin's red face showed that he was agitated when he jumped in. "Wayne and Ryan said they weren't going to walk home, and now look. Since I'm in the car, there they go running down the road. They just didn't want me to walk with them," Kevin said angrily. "That wasn't nice, was it, Mother?"

Mother had seen clearly what had happened. "No, it wasn't," she replied. "But don't let it bother you. Don't be a silly goose and snap at the tires." Mom smiled, then continued. "You cannot change their behavior by getting angry, Kevin. If you show them you are upset, then they'll be satisfied that they hurt you. And you'll be doing wrong by showing anger. You need to ask Jesus to help you not be upset. If they don't get a reaction from you, they won't think their meanness was so much fun after all."

"Well, I'm going to just ignore it. And I'll try to be nice to them tomorrow," Kevin said. "I won't be a silly goose and snap at their bad behavior."

The next morning Kevin called out good morning to Wayne and Vince, but they did not answer. When the school bell rang Kevin got busy with a morning of math and reading lessons. During the lunch break the teacher stepped out of the room to answer the phone. Lunchtime without the teacher's presence was always a challenge for Kevin. Wayne and Vince were sure to try to get him into trouble in some way. Their daring him to do something dumb was becoming routine, and Kevin was starting to wonder why he called them friends.

"Dare you to toss your carrots into the trash," Wayne

challenged Kevin.

"Wayne, you throw yours in first," Kevin demanded.

"Oh, come on, Kevin. Don't be a coward," Vince whispered loudly. "You do it first, and then we will do it. Quick, before the teacher comes back!"

"You both always say that, but then you never do it or get into trouble," replied Kevin. *This time I'll stand on my own two feet like Mother is always telling me to do. I won't let them push me into trouble,* Kevin thought.

"Did you ever see such a chicken?" Wayne said to Vince.

That was all it took!

Swish! Plunk! The carrots landed on top of the trash. Kevin couldn't stand being called a chicken!

"Now it's your turn to toss yours in," Kevin commanded, angry and disgusted with himself more than his tormentors.

"My mother wouldn't like it if I threw my vegetables away," Wayne said with a smirk.

"Neither would mine," said Vince, snickering.

Kevin had had enough. He got up and walked outside. He didn't even feel like eating the rest of his lunch. Those fellows were always getting him to do something he knew he shouldn't do!

After school the teacher called him aside. "Kevin, did you throw your carrots into the trash?" she asked.

"Yes, I did, because Wayne and Vince told me to and said they would throw their vegetables in also, but they didn't!" Kevin replied.

"Why do you think you must do what they tell you to do

when it is wrong? Surely you don't throw away good food like that at home," Miss Carla observed.

"No, we don't throw away good food . . . but, Miss Carla, those fellows are always daring me to do things," Kevin answered lamely. "And . . . and they call me chicken if I don't."

"So how does being called a chicken actually hurt you? It only hurts when we are proud. Really, when you do the wrong things they tell you to do, you are hurting yourself more than the name 'Chicken' could ever hurt you. 'No' is one of the hardest words to say, but one of the most important words in the dictionary," Miss Carla finished with a smile.

Kevin's waiting mother saw his troubled face as he got into the car. "How was your day?" she asked.

"I made a dumb choice again," Kevin answered, telling his mother what had happened. "I hate being called a chicken."

"So what do you think would solve your problem—courage or knowledge?" Mother asked, readily guessing the problem.

"I need courage to say 'no' when I want to say 'yes.' I need courage to do right—in spite of being called a chicken," Kevin replied with a sigh.

> The foolishness of man perverteth his way: and his heart fretteth against the Lord.
> Proverbs 19:3

"I've been acting as silly as a goose," he continued, hanging his head. "Just like those geese running after our tires, which could squash them in a second, I run after Wayne and Vince and they squash me every time. I think I need to ask God to help me stand on my own two feet."

"And I believe my son is doing some wise thinking," Mother said with a smile.

A Broken Leg and a Merry Heart

The phone rang and Shanita answered. "Hello, this is Shanita."

"Hi, Shanita. Have you heard what happened to Danielle?" Brenda asked. "I thought you probably hadn't heard since you were out of town."

"No! I hope it's nothing bad," replied Shanita.

"Well, it is bad. She broke her leg and is at home in a cast!" Brenda exclaimed. "She's not supposed to walk at all for a couple of weeks."

"How did she break her leg?" asked Shanita.

"Her mother sent her to the store. It was almost dark and she was in a hurry. She tripped over a wire strung across the sidewalk," Brenda explained.

"Well, who would be watching for a wire over the sidewalk?

That's no place for a wire!" Shanita exclaimed. "That's a foolish trick for someone to play."

"Yes, and today at school I heard the boys say who they thought did it. I guess I'd better not repeat the name since no one knows for sure," Brenda said.

"That's a perfect example of 'feet being swift in running to mischief,' like our memory verse last week from Proverbs 6," Shanita said. "When a boy—it probably was a boy—does something so foolish, he likely isn't thinking ahead as to how it might hurt someone. He is only thinking of his fun and how smart he is to think of such a trick.

The heart knoweth his own bitterness; and a stranger doth not intermeddle with his joy. Proverbs 14:10

"Our foolishness—I think we girls can act foolishly too sometimes—is when we go our own way and do our own thing. We forget we may hurt someone or be very unkind in the process," Brenda added.

"Yes, that is so true." The girls were quiet as they pondered a bit.

"Back to Danielle and her injury—we should do something nice for her," Shanita said. "Why don't you come to my house after school tomorrow and we can decide what we can do and when to visit her."

"Oh, that is a good idea. Two heads are better than one," Brenda replied with a laugh. "I'll meet you after school under the oak tree and we can walk to your house together."

○ ○ ○ ○ ○ ○ ○ ○ ○ ○ ○ ○ ○ ○ ○

A few days later as Brenda and Shanita approached Danielle's house for their planned visit, they each carried a lovely gift bag. But they were a little nervous now that it came down to actually carrying out their plan.

"Do you think Danielle will be glad to see us? She might be in too much pain to be cheerful," Brenda said.

"Well, if she doesn't feel much like seeing us, we don't have to stay long," replied Shanita.

Mrs. Wilson met the girls at the door. "Oh, do come in," she invited. "Danielle will be so delighted to see you. She's been saying she wishes some of her friends would come by. She's in the living room on the couch."

"Oh, girls, come in," Danielle welcomed. "It is so lovely that you have come. Have chairs! Do stay awhile. I'm tired of staying indoors—I'd like to hear the outside news. What's going on at school?"

"Not a lot," said Brenda. "Did you hear that Judy's dog got hit and killed by a car? Someone said it looked like the driver deliberately hit the dog."

"Oh, no! How sad for Judy!" Danielle said. "Bimbo was her constant companion."

"She wasn't at school for the past three days. Someone said she cried herself sick. I can't imagine crying over a dog that much," Brenda said.

"Maybe you could if you had lost your father a year ago, and your mother had to work, and you were left alone a lot.

Remember, Judy has no brothers or sisters like you and I have," Shanita reminded.

"Well, when you put it all that way, I guess it looks like a bigger deal than I thought," Brenda replied. "Our teacher suggested that we all bring money and see if we can collect enough for her to buy another dog."

"That would be nice," Danielle smiled. "I would like to send some money for that project. I'm sure Mother will let me. But it will take a while for a new dog to take Bimbo's place. He was such a smart dog and very protective of Judy. He was a good companion. It must be really hard for Judy."

"Yes, I'm sure you are right, but I don't think I could love a dog as much as she does," Brenda answered. Then she continued more slowly and thoughtfully, "Maybe I could if I had no brothers or sisters."

"And if you had no Cotton Candy," Shanita added with a laugh. "If something happened to that cat I think you would stay home from school too."

"Oh, don't even mention something happening to Candy!" Brenda exclaimed. "I couldn't bear it. I guess I'm just as attached to my cat as Judy was to her dog. I never thought about it that way."

"Well, I love my baby sister, Elaina, more than I could love a cat or dog," Shanita said. "We each have someone or some pet that is special to us. And we need to respect each other's special feelings. Mother always says I must never make fun of someone just because I don't feel the same way about the same thing."

"That is very true—and I am sorry for making Judy's feelings

Sometimes Mirrors Lie

about her dog sound silly. I really wasn't thinking beyond my nose, as *my* mother says sometimes," Brenda replied with a smile.

"Well, here we are chattering about Judy and Bimbo, but I want to hear how you are doing, Danielle," Brenda said.

"Yes," Shanita added. "Tell us how you are feeling. Do you have a lot of pain? Did you find out yet who put that wire across the sidewalk?"

> A merry heart doeth good like a medicine: but a broken spirit drieth the bones.
>
> Proverbs 17:22

"I really don't know who did it and I don't want to know," answered Danielle. "Someone just made a foolish decision and . . ." Danielle hesitated.

"You are suffering because of it," broke in Brenda. "It is not right for us to make someone else suffer."

"But we all hurt someone at times—even unintentionally—and we must be forgiving," Danielle replied. "As to my leg, yes, I have some pain and I kind of hurt all over. I feel like I need some exercise but the doctor says not yet. It was a bad break and will take a long time to heal. But I am so thankful I didn't break my wrist or arm. This way I can still do some things. But say, I'd like to see what is in your bags," she said, changing the subject.

"They are *your* bags," Shanita said, laughing.

"Oh, my, what a lot you brought me!" Danielle exclaimed as she began pulling out the gifts. "Cookies, candy, some fruit and paints, a drawing book, a doily to embroider, a craft to make, and a game. Oh, we must try this game right now; you girls can teach me."

And so the girls played the new game until it was time for them to leave. "We really must go," Shanita announced, looking at her watch. "I need to stop in to see my grandma yet tonight."

"Please come again," Danielle said. "It's been so much fun having you here. And thank you for all the gifts! I am anxious to embroider the doily for my bedroom. Thank you again and again! I'm so glad my arm isn't broken! I can still embroider and draw."

As the girls parted, Brenda marveled, "It's so amazing how happy Danielle can be with her broken leg and the pain and having to stay inside and everything."

"Don't you think it's because she always finds something to be thankful for?" Shanita asked.

"Yes, that's probably it. Her merry heart is like good medicine for her attitude and for her healing. I doubt that I would feel thankful for anything if I were in her shoes," Brenda said.

"She can't even wear her own shoe right now!" Shanita quipped. And the two friends shared a laugh.

A Finger and Foolishness

True story

"Lyndal, why do you always have a bunch of boys hanging around here?" Allison asked.

"Because I enjoy company—the more the better," Lyndal replied. "We have lots of fun. Just because you can handle only one friend doesn't mean I can't have more. Anyway, you shouldn't be complaining—your friend Tonya almost lives here."

"Well, her home is such a shanty and she loves being here," Allison said. "Since her mother died, it's hard for her to be at home. Her dad isn't much company."

"Yeah, I guess I can't blame her. But just let me have my friends and you can have yours," Lyndal replied as he disappeared out the door. Soon four neighbor boys joined him for a game of football out in the field.

A short time later the doorbell rang and Allison hurried to the door. It was Tonya.

"Hi, can you go on a walk with me?" Tonya asked. "We need to talk about that map project for school."

"That's right! It's due next week. I'll ask Mom and be back in a minute," Allison replied.

The way of a fool is right in his own eyes: but he that hearkeneth unto counsel is wise. Proverbs 12:15

The girls made plans for their project as they walked. After a while they headed back to Allison's house.

"Oh, no, the yard is full of boys again . . . Well, not quite full," Allison corrected herself. "Let's sneak around and go in the back door."

The girls were almost around the back corner of the house when Lyndal spotted his sister.

"Hey, Allison, bring us some of your delicious chocolate chip cookies," he called. "But don't bring any of those burned ones."

"I'll put some on a plate, but you can come in and get them yourself," Allison called back.

"That's my sister for you—sassy, smart, and spirited." Lyndal laughed loudly.

Allison put some cookies on a paper plate and set them on the kitchen counter. Then she and Tonya disappeared into her bedroom.

She plopped down on her bed. "That brother of mine is so exasperating and embarrassing. The more friends he has around him the more foolish he acts. I'm sure he won't tell the boys why the cookies burned."

"What happened?" Tonya asked, smiling.

"It's really not funny. He held my bedroom door shut and I couldn't go out when the timer on the stove was ringing. It's his fault the cookies got burned, not mine! But all his friends will think I'm a real dummy."

"Does it really matter what they think?" Tonya asked. "Anyway, he said you were smart. You take things too seriously, and overreact."

"Well, you just don't know how it is to have a brother who constantly torments you," Allison said. "But maybe you're right. I suppose I shouldn't care so much what those boys think of me. And I do get too upset by Lyndal's teasing."

o o o o o o o o o o o o o o

It was a rainy day—and what was there for an active fellow to do? Mother had said, "No other boys today. I want you to entertain yourself."

Lyndal was fiddling around with his little bow and arrow in his bedroom. It was just a harmless toy left over from his fourth birthday, long ago.

Taking the bow and an arrow with a suction cup tip, he headed for the kitchen where he heard his sister putting away dishes.

"Want to see how good a shot I am?" he called from the doorway.

Allison turned, and when she saw Lyndal with the bow and arrow she took off running. That was just what Lyndal wanted—some excitement! Around and around, through the kitchen, the dining room, and down the hall they went.

Allison began yelling, "Mother, Mother, Lyndal is chasing me with . . ." Suddenly she screamed, "Oh, ouch, my finger, my finger!"

She had just started another run through the kitchen when her left hand hit the edge of the refrigerator as she rounded the corner. Yelping in pain, she stared down at her little finger, which was sticking out at a strange angle.

Lyndal was right behind her. When he saw the ugly angle of her little finger, his face turned white. "Oh, Allison, I didn't mean to hurt you. Here, sit down and I'll go find Mother."

Mother hurried up from the basement. After hearing Allison's story and taking a look at the finger, she turned to Lyndal. "You go to your room and stay there," she told him in no uncertain terms. "I want you to do some serious thinking while I take Allison to the emergency room."

Lyndal waited and waited. Why were they taking so long? Would she need an operation that would cost a lot of money? Or was something else broken?

Perhaps, he thought, he should stop teasing his sister so much. But why did she always overreact? That was what made it so much fun. She should have known he couldn't hurt her with that little bow. Finally he heard the car drive in.

He went to the door to meet them. "Was it broken?"

Allison smiled, but she had a cast on her little finger. "Of course it was broken," she said. "And now I can tell everyone that my brother broke my finger."

"I didn't break it. You broke it by running into the fridge,"

Lyndal replied. "There was no need for you to act so scared." Then he added with a grin, "But I suppose I could take some responsibility for helping to get it broken!"

"Indeed you will," Mother said. "You will need to get several more mowing jobs to help pay for the emergency room visit. Perhaps that will help you remember not to act so foolishly."

"Yes, I guess I should stop teasing my little sister," Lyndal agreed.

"I'm not little! I'm bigger than you are!" Allison exclaimed.

"I'll be taller than you one of these days," Lyndal declared.

"I expect you will, little brother," said Allison with a smile.

Little did she realize how true her words were. As the years passed, "little brother" grew to be six foot, four inches tall—and he grew a bit wiser too.

Snoopy or Curious?

Based on a true incident

The phone lay on the stand beside the girls' bed. Suddenly Shari heard a soft ringing. *Oh, that must be Jolynn's phone. I wonder why she has the volume set so soft.* Shari picked up the phone and saw that a text had come. She quickly read the message.

Hi, Jo! What time @ Arby's on Sat. for Shari's bday?

Oh, dear, I suppose that wasn't meant for me to read. Shari dropped the phone and left the room to go about her own business. If she kept quiet, Jolynn would never know she had read the text. *Well, I guess I ruined that surprise,* she thought in dismay.

At the breakfast table the next morning Mother was planning her week. "And on Saturday we need to clean out the greenhouse and get it ready for winter."

"I can't help . . ." Shari stopped mid-sentence and Jolynn gave her a questioning look.

"Sure, you all will help," Mother said and continued with her plans.

As soon as the girls were alone, Jolynn asked, "Did you snoop and read my phone?"

"Um-m-m, yes, I did. I had no idea . . ."

"You had no business with my phone!" Jolynn said. "You are so snoopy! I have half a notion to just cancel the plans!"

"Oh, please, Jolynn, don't. I almost never get to go to Arby's. And to go to lunch with you and Crystal would be so special."

"But you have spoiled all the *special* about it! It was to be a surprise. You are like the fool in Proverbs, always meddling into other's business," Jolynn replied, almost with tears.

"Oh, Jolynn, I am so sorry. Truly I am. Please forgive me." Shari gave her sister a hug.

"I forgive you, Shari, but I am disappointed."

The week went by slowly for Shari. One day she heard a text come in on Dad's phone. She walked by the phone, looking the other way. She did not pick it up. But why were cell phones so tempting?

On Thursday Shari arrived home from school all excited.

"Mom!" she called as the door slammed behind her. "Do you know what we're going to do next Wednesday?"

"No, I don't. What is it?" Mom wondered as she bagged a loaf of fresh bread.

"Mr. Bender said our class is going to do something fun!" Shari gave a whoop as she dived into the pantry with her empty lunch box. "He said it is a surprise. I like surprises when they are good ones!"

From the pantry, Shari heard a soft *pa-link* from the kitchen. "Mom, you got a text! May I look at it?"

Mom was slicing bread with an electric knife and had not heard her cell phone. "No, remember I told you not to mess with my phone. Please empty the dishwasher now."

Shari pulled open the dishwasher and stuck a few glasses into the cupboard. As she sorted the silverware into the slots in the drawer, she glanced at the counter.

There was Mom's cell phone. *I wonder what that text is about. Maybe it's about what we're going to do on Wednesday.* Shari's fingers were on the phone.

"Mom!" Shari yelled. "We are going biking on Wednesday! And it's for my birthday! Oh, I'm so glad! I can't wait!"

Mom looked up with a frown. "Shari, I told you not to look at that text!"

"But Mom, it was right there when I touched the phone! I couldn't help but see it!"

"You shouldn't have touched the phone in the first place. Now that you disobeyed me, the surprise is spoiled. Think of how much fun it would have been to walk into school and find out you are going biking for your birthday! And think of how the teachers will feel when they find out you already know about the biking. It will be disappointing for them!"

Shari's face fell. She stared at the floor.

"You already spoiled Jolynn's surprise—and now this. I have told you before not to look at my cell phone. Now, I want you to fold the laundry all by yourself, because you disobeyed.

"And you must learn to stop meddling in other people's business. You need to control your curiosity. You have hurt others' feelings by snooping in their stuff."

Shari didn't like the word *snooping—curiosity* sounded better. Why had God had given her so much curiosity? It was always getting her into trouble. Mother had told her curiosity is a good teacher. If she was curious about good things she could learn many interesting things about herself and the world around her. But when she was snooping into other people's business was when she got into trouble. *I guess I can see the difference when I really want to,* Shari admitted to herself.

"Yes, Mother, you're right. I will try harder to control my curiosity," she promised.

⦾ ⦾ ⦾ ⦾ ⦾ ⦾ ⦾ ⦾ ⦾ ⦾ ⦾ ⦾ ⦾ ⦾ ⦾

The school year seemed to fly by and soon it was time for the school trip. They always went to interesting places and had a picnic and lots of fun.

One evening Shari heard the *pa-link* of her dad's phone. She walked past it and saw the words "school trip" and now she was really curious. She quickly read the message and hurried back to her job of setting the table and pouring water for supper.

At the table Dad talked to the children about how they should behave when they went on the field trip. "And I do not want you children asking 'Why?' when you see a couple of the boys are not present."

Without thinking, Shari spoke up, "Oh, I know. Nathan and Brent cannot go on the field trip because they lied to the teacher."

Dad looked hard at Shari and asked, "How do you know anything about it?"

Shari's face turned red and she hung her head, saying nothing.

"Tell me, Shari, how you know," Dad said firmly.

"I-I read the text—ah—on your cell phone," Shari admitted.

Dad looked at the other children and said, "I don't want any of you repeating those names or saying what happened. Do you understand? This problem is none of your business."

"Yes, Dad," they promised.

"And you, Shari, may not go on the field trip. Somehow you must learn the lesson of keeping your nose in your own business."

It is an honour for a man to cease from strife: but every fool will be meddling.
Proverbs 20:3

A gasp came from Shari and tears ran down her cheeks. Did Dad really mean she couldn't go on the field trip? She looked up into his face and knew he meant what he had said.

"We have talked to you many times, Shari, about this snooping business—and it hasn't improved a whole lot. We need to see a change. I don't want my lovely girl to grow into a snoopy young lady."

Shari knew she had hurt others with her snooping, but this time she had received the biggest hurt. She determined to break her bad habit of curiosity and call it what it was—snooping!

—Sabrina Miller

Snoopy or Curious?

Just-a-Minute Judy

It was a new school year and Judy was still adjusting to her new teacher. *Miss Miller seems rather strict,* Judy observed. *I will be so glad when I can graduate from eighth grade. Ha! Here I am thinking about graduating and we have barely started the year.*

Judy pulled her social studies book from her desk—her favorite subject. She was absorbed in her reading when the teacher called, "Judy, will you please come to my desk?"

Without thinking, Judy replied, "In just a minute." When she looked up from her book five minutes later she noticed many faces turned toward her—some smiling in amusement, others anxious. Why were they looking at her so strangely? She looked back down at her book and began reading again.

"Judy, I asked you to come to my desk," the teacher said

firmly. "I want you to come here—now."

Quickly Judy walked to the teacher's desk. Miss Miller handed her a math paper and explained, "I want you to correct this math lesson before recess." Then more quietly she said, "I will talk with you at recess."

After the children were dismissed, Judy sat in her desk,

Sometimes Mirrors Lie

waiting. Miss Miller came and sat at the desk across the aisle. She turned toward her student and waited for Judy to meet her gaze. "Judy," she said, "I do not want you to say 'just a minute' to me again. When I call you I expect you to come promptly."

"Yes, ma'am—I mean, yes, Miss Miller."

"You may go outside now," Miss Miller said.

Miss Miller walked along outside and watched as the children played. She heard Lyle call, "Run, Just-a-minute Judy. Run, Just-a-minute Judy!" Why was he calling her Just-a-minute Judy? Then Miss Miller heard Sharon call, "Just-a-minute Judy."

Miss Miller did not appreciate nicknames and especially not this one. By the end of the day she had decided what she would do. She gave her class what she called a "pep talk." She told her students clearly that she wanted to hear no nicknames. Then she added seriously, "That includes Just-a-minute Judy." She finished with a smile, but the students knew she meant what she said.

○ ○ ○ ○ ○ ○ ○ ○ ○ ○ ○ ○ ○ ○ ○

"Mom," Judy said when she arrived home that afternoon, "Miss Miller certainly does not like nicknames. She said the children must stop calling me Just-a-minute Judy."

"Well, that makes me happy," Mom said. "Maybe that will help you to stop saying 'just a minute.' "

The next day Judy tried very hard not to say "just a minute," but just after the last break she was reading a library book when Miss Miller called her to her desk.

"Just a minute," Judy said. Then she realized what she had

done. She quickly jumped from her desk and walked up to the teacher. "I'm sorry. I forgot. I guess I have a bad habit."

"Yes, indeed! Will you please pass out these papers, Judy?" She handed her a small stack. "Thank you. And I want to see you after school."

Judy took the papers from the teacher. Her hands were shaking. What was the teacher going to do? She glanced down at the papers. Oh, they were copies of a poem.

After Judy had given each student a copy, Miss Miller said to the class, "Before you all go home today I want us to read together this poem on habits, and then we are going to memorize it. I heard some of you using nicknames again today. This is a habit we want to break. Okay, together, let's read."

Habits

A habit is a sticky thing;
Much good or evil it can bring;
It binds a victim, holds him fast,
And keeps him in a viselike grasp.

Bad habits grow with extra speed,
Much like a healthy growing weed.
The roots grow deep, the stem grows stout;
How difficult to pull it out!

Good habits are a little slow;
They need a lot of care to grow;
If tended well, they grow more fair
Than any bloom a plant can bear.

Good habits help us all through life;
Bad habits bring us pain and strife;
Our habits, whether right or wrong,
Each day will grow more firm and strong.

—Carol Beachy Wenger

After school Judy sat in her desk waiting for her teacher.

"You have read the poem," Miss Miller told her, "and we are going to memorize it. But right now I want you to write it three times, to help you remember the habit you need to get rid of."

Reluctantly, Judy pulled out her tablet and began to write, "A habit is a sticky thing . . ."

o o o o o o o o o o o o o o

"You are late coming home," Mother remarked.

"Yes, I had to stay after school and copy a poem three times because I said 'just a minute,' " Judy said tiredly. "Miss Miller is so strict!"

"Judy, she is only trying to help you," Mother reminded.

"I suppose so," Judy answered, "but I'll be so glad when this week is over."

On Saturday morning Judy felt it was time to relax in her room and do what she wanted to do.

But soon she heard Mother call from downstairs. "Judy, please bring the dirty clothes from your hamper. I want to wash this morning."

"Yes, Mother. I'll be there in just a minute," Judy called.

Ten minutes later Judy dumped her dirty clothes on the laundry room floor.

"Where have you been?" Mother asked.

"Oh, I was just finishing a picture I was painting," answered Judy as she headed upstairs.

A while later Mother called again. "Judy, will you please scrub the bathroom sink and sweep the living room carpet? Aunt Sue is coming today."

"Sure, Mom. Just a minute," Judy answered absentmindedly.

"I want it done right now before Aunt Sue comes," Mother said. Hearing no reply, she went about her work with a knowing look. Judy was really slackening in her efforts to break her bad habit.

Half an hour later the doorbell rang. Instead of running to the door as usual, Judy ran to the bathroom and quickly started scrubbing the sink. There wasn't time to sweep the carpet now that Aunt Sue was here.

As Judy came into the living room, Mother and Aunt Sue were talking.

"I thought maybe Judy would like to ride the bus back into town with me. I'd like to take her to a new museum that just opened," Aunt Sue said, looking from Mother to Judy.

"Oh, may I, Mother? I love to go anywhere with Aunt Sue," Judy said excitedly.

"We'll have to see," Mother replied. "Now go and straighten your room and change into clean clothes while I talk with Aunt Sue. But remember, at twelve o'clock sharp I want the table set for lunch. Aunt Sue wants to leave on the one o'clock bus.

Be careful to watch your clock."

"Oh, I will, Mother," Judy said happily as she went to her room. On her desk at the bottom of a pile of books she found *Heidi*.

"Oh, there's that book!" she exclaimed. "I had only four or five chapters to finish. Let's see—it's only 11:00, so I have plenty of time to read and finish my room."

Soon Judy was snuggled into her big armchair following Heidi and Peter and the goats over the Swiss mountain trails.

In the kitchen Mother had started preparing lunch. It was fifteen minutes before 12:00. Perhaps she should give Judy a reminder. She would hate to ruin Aunt Sue's plans for the day.

"Judy," Mother called. "You have just a few minutes until it's time to set the table. You'd better come, wash your hands, and be ready to set the table."

"Okay, Mom, I'll be there in just a minute," Judy replied.

Mom and Aunt Sue looked at each other.

As the clock struck twelve, Aunt Sue placed two plates and glasses and some silverware on the table. Mom and Aunt Sue sat down to lunch alone.

"I'm afraid we'd better not wait for Judy," Mother said. "It's hard to tell when her *minute* might be up. Her minutes seem to be getting longer and longer."

After prayer, Mom and Aunt Sue chatted, but Judy was upstairs, lost in dreams on the Swiss Alps.

"I'll have to leave now if I want to catch the 1:00 bus. But I guess I could wait for the 1:30 bus," Aunt Sue said, looking questioningly at Mother.

"No, you should take the 1:00 bus," Mother replied. "I think Judy is going to learn a hard but needed lesson this time. She must learn to be prompt in obedience. I don't think she'll be 'Just-a-minute Judy' after this."

Aunt Sue left, quiet and disappointed. She thought Judy had been excited about going with her, but her niece certainly didn't act like it.

Ten minutes later Judy came skipping down the steps. She stopped short when she saw the dirty plates on the table. "Mom? Aunt Sue? Did you eat without me? Sorry, I lost track of the time."

Mom appeared in the kitchen doorway. "Aunt Sue needed to leave to catch the 1:00 bus. She could not wait another minute."

"She left without me!" Judy wailed as the truth sank in. "Oh, Mom!"

Three weeks passed before Aunt Sue arrived at Judy's house on another beautiful Saturday morning. She hoped things would go better this time.

When the doorbell rang, Judy ran to the front door. Before Aunt Sue even set foot inside, Judy blurted, "Oh, Aunt Sue, I am so sorry. I was so disappointed not to be able to go with you to the new museum, but it was my own fault. I am really working hard to break my just-a-minute habit."

Aunt Sue smiled as she stepped inside; she was sure things would go differently today. "I came to see if my favorite niece wanted to go to that new museum today."

"Well, first I must ask you to forgive me for the way I behaved the last time."

Sometimes Mirrors Lie

"Yes, most certainly!"

Mother stepped into the living room, "Welcome, Sue. I am glad to see you. After what happened the last time you were here, I wasn't sure when you would return."

"Oh, we already have that all patched up," Aunt Sue replied, and then she told Mother why she had come.

"So you're willing to try again," Mother said. "I feel like I have a new daughter—and I'm sure things will go differently today." Turning to Judy she said, "You may go upstairs and get ready to go."

Judy ran up the stairs with a whoop. And Sue asked, "So what was the turning point?"

Mother replied, "Missing that trip to the museum really made Judy try harder to break her bad habit. But I think her teacher also gets a lot of credit.

Seest thou a man diligent in his business? he shall stand before kings; he shall not stand before mean men. Proverbs 22:29

"Miss Miller absolutely would not allow her to say 'just a minute' like her teacher did last year. She also had Judy memorize a poem about habits. That poem helped her to see the importance of good habits. Then Miss Miller gave her students an assignment—writing a short essay on diligence. That seemed to really help Judy see the seriousness of her problem."

Soon Judy came flying down the stairs, holding a paper in her hand. "Mother, would it be okay if I read my essay to Aunt Sue?"

"Yes, I think that would be a good reminder for all of us," Mother said.

"Well, here it is.

Diligence

Diligence is doing what you should do even when you don't feel like doing it. Diligence is coming the instant you are called. Diligence is putting down your book when there is another job to do. Diligence is being obedient, careful, thoughtful, attentive, and persistent in whatever you are asked to do."

"Excellent," Aunt Sue said. "Now, if we leave this early, we can have lunch together at the restaurant before we go to the museum."

"Oh, that sounds great, Aunt Sue!" Judy exclaimed. "I'm ready to go this very second."

Jake the Fake

True story

"Jake, I think you are well enough to wash dishes this morning," Mother said. Jake had been sick and had missed his turn washing dishes the past three days. Now it was Saturday.

"Do I have to wash them this morning?" Jake moaned. "Do I really have to do *all* these dishes?" Mother had done some baking and there were a few extra dishes this morning. Jake knew he sounded like a whining three-year-old, but just now he didn't care.

Ever since his sisters had gotten jobs away from home, Jake and his brother needed to take turns helping with the break-fast dishes. Normally Jake washed dishes without much comment. He knew it was his usual job. But it didn't take too many "extras" to make the job look like a mountain when Jake had his "I-don't-want-to-do-this-job" attitude.

"It's really not such a big job once you get them all neatly stacked together," Mother encouraged. "Just hurry a little and it won't take long."

"But my head hurts." Jake leaned his elbow on the cupboard and propped his head in his hand, a forlorn look in his big brown eyes.

"Jake, you've had a long vacation from washing dishes. You seemed to be feeling fine this morning, and I don't think it is going to hurt you to wash these dishes. Now get busy," Mother finished firmly.

Carelessly Jake started pulling the dishes from the sink and putting them on the counter beside the dirty bowls and pans. Suddenly he shouted, "Mother, come! There's water everywhere! I don't know where it came from."

Mother hurried to his side. "Jake, you need to empty the dirty water from the dishes before you put them on the counter. You just don't want to do this job, so you're being careless," Mother said.

She got a dish towel and handed it to Jake. "Now you wipe up that water on the counter top and the floor. There is no need for such a mess. And dry the cupboard door too. You know how to do the job right. You have made yourself a lot of extra work."

Jake wiped up the water and finished cleaning out the sink. Slowly he got out the dishpan, opened the faucet, and started filling the pan. He squirted soap into the dishpan and played in the suds. He washed a plate and grumbled. He washed a few cups and mumbled. Ever so slowly he washed, complaining all the while.

"Do I have to wash them all? I don't feel good. I'm getting sick," he said with a whine.

Finally Mother said, "Jake, if you're sick, go to bed!"

"I'll just go lie on the couch," Jake replied.

"No, sick boys belong in bed," Mother said, "and no books to read. If you are sick, close your eyes and rest."

Jake washed a few more dishes. Suddenly he started to cry. "My stomach hurts. I'm sick."

Mother came to his side. "Okay, if you're sick, you must go to bed and stay there the rest of the morning."

Slowly Jake went to his room.

"Don't you think you should give him something for his stomach?" Father asked as he came into the kitchen just in time to hear the last part of the conversation.

"I don't think he is really sick," Mother replied. She quickly pushed the silverware and a few other dishes into the dishpan so they could soak. Then she went about her other work.

Barely five minutes later Jake appeared in the kitchen with a sheepish grin.

"May I finish the dishes now?" he asked.

"Sure, go ahead," Mother answered.

"Say, what happened to you?" Father called from the living room. "Did your stomach get healed in the bedroom?"

Jake simply grinned as he quickly finished the dishes.

Later Mother told Jake, "I think your I-don't-want-to-do-this-job attitude is what made you feel sick. When you decided you'd rather wash dishes than stay in bed, you started feeling well."

○ ○ ○ ○ ○ ○ ○ ○ ○ ○ ○ ○ ○ ○

"After breakfast, Jake," Dad said several days later, "I want you to clean out under the rabbit cages. Please haul their fertilizer to that compost pile in the corner of the garden."

"But Dad, that is so far to haul it! Can't I put it behind the shed?" Jake's face wrinkled into a huge frown. "It will take a lot less time to put it behind the shed."

"And it will do a lot less good behind the shed! It would have to be moved later. I want it in the garden," Dad said firmly.

"Can't Carlin help me?" Jake groaned. "He's not doing anything,"

"Carlin is in the shop getting the lawn mower ready. He has his job and you have yours."

"He always gets the fun, easy jobs," Jake mumbled.

"I want to hear no more complaining. Out to the rabbit pens you go—with a smile! Remember you're the owner of the rabbits."

Jake gave Dad a half smile and headed toward the rabbits. With the wheelbarrow and shovel he soon had one pile cleaned up. Then he started pushing the wheelbarrow toward the garden. Such hard work!

Suddenly Jake stepped into a hollow in the ground and almost lost his balance. *Wow, that was a close one. I almost dumped the wheelbarrow. What a mess that would be if I had*

Sometimes Mirrors Lie

spilled it. I've got to find Dad and tell him I just can't do this job. I need help. I almost sprained my ankle.

Jake left the wheelbarrow and limped toward the shop where Dad was working. Carlin saw him and called out, "Hey, Jake the Fake, where are you going? Why are you limping?" Carlin had shut off the mower and was cleaning out the grass catcher.

"Dad told you not to call me Jake the Fake!" Jake exclaimed. He headed into the shop.

"Well, what is your problem, son?" Dad asked, looking at Jake.

Put away from thee a froward [dishonest] mouth, and perverse [corrupt] lips put far from thee.

Proverbs 4:24

"I-I almost twisted my ankle and my leg hurts, and I almost dumped the wheelbarrow on the drive. The job is too hard for me," Jake whined.

"Well, don't put so much in the wheelbarrow and it will be easier to push," Dad suggested.

"Small loads would take me forever. I-I really need to go into the house and rest my leg," Jake said.

"Did you actually twist your ankle?" Dad asked kindly.

"Ah . . . I guess not. The job is just too hard and Carlin called me Jake the Fake, and you told him not to," Jake complained.

"I think your problem really is the I-don't-want-to attitude," Dad said. "I'm sure you are able to do the job if you just take small loads to the garden. Remember, 'A bad attitude is like a flat tire, you can't get anywhere until you change it.'"

Jake's scowl slowly changed to a grin. He had heard that

quote before. "I will try," he answered.

"Another thing to remember, son, is that it is a serious thing to be deceitful. God is truth and in Him is no darkness. Deceit is darkness. Satan is a liar and the father of deceit and hypocrisy. If we are going to be servants of God, we must be truthful, pure, and open. I'm sure you don't like being called Jake the Fake, so don't play the part of a fake!"

Dirty Socks and Friendly Wounds

True story

"Kenton, have you put your dirty socks into the wash?" Mother called from the laundry room.

"No, not yet," Kenton called back.

"Well, you need to do it right now," Mother said.

"I am making my sandwich for my lunch," replied Kenton.

Ten minutes later Mother called again, "Kenton! You need to bring your dirty socks now."

"I'm just on my way outside to feed the dog and cat," Kenton called back again.

Mother sighed, wondering when Kenton would make getting his dirty socks to the wash a priority. If he would just learn to put them into the hamper with his other dirty clothes, they would get washed.

Kenton rushed back into the house, put on his coat, and grabbed his lunch pail.

"Kenton, where are your dirty socks?" Mother asked. "'Action is the key. Do it immediately,'" she quoted.

"But Mother, the bus is here. I must go." And out the door he went.

"Well, he put on his last pair of clean socks this morning. I wonder what he will do tomorrow morning," Mother said to herself.

○ ○ ○ ○ ○ ○ ○ ○ ○ ○ ○ ○ ○ ○ ○

Kenton searched and searched for a clean pair of socks. There were absolutely no clean socks in any of his drawers. How could he have forgotten again to put them in the wash? There were socks under his bed. There were socks under his desk. There were socks under his dresser. There were even socks stuffed into his shoes, but they were all dirty. Finally he resorted to a dirty pair, put on his shoes, and ran for the bus. Was it his imagination, or could he really smell his feet?

Halfway through the school day he noticed Shana in the next row of desks, sitting with a Kleenex over her nose. Half an hour later she was still holding her nose. Then the teacher noticed and asked, "Shana, do you have a bloody nose or a cold?"

Shana glanced in Kenton's direction and said quietly, "Something smells bad over here."

At least she didn't say she smelled dirty feet, Kenton thought gratefully, but his face reddened.

"Kenton, do you know what is causing the smell?" the teacher asked.

Kenton simply shrugged. He felt like he could not answer. Then Brad, sitting in front of him, turned around and nodded his head as if to say, "It is you who stinks."

Faithful are the wounds of a friend; but the kisses of an enemy are deceitful.

Proverbs 27:6

When the final bell of the day rang, Kenton hurried to the bus. He did not feel like talking to anyone. He put his books and lunch box on the seat beside him, hoping no one would try to sit there. Brad sat down in the seat in front of Kenton.

"I say, ol' chap, are you wearing dirty socks?" Brad asked as he turned around and grinned at Kenton. Then, seeing Kenton's red face, he added, "Don't worry, sometimes I forget to put my socks in the wash too."

Kenton kept his head turned, looking intently out the bus window but not seeing anything. He felt greatly relieved when the bus arrived at his house. Quickly he hurried to the house and went to his room, intending to gather all his dirty socks. But when he saw the model car on his desk, he decided to work on it for a while.

When Kenton finally went out to the kitchen his mother asked, "Where have you been? Did you forget about a snack? How was your day?"

"That's three questions to answer," Kenton laughed. It felt so good to be away from school. "I went straight to my room.

I was going to pick up dirty socks—but I was working on my model instead. I didn't forget my snack . . . that's why I'm here now. And my day in school was terrible with smelly, dirty socks."

"So your dirty socks caught up with you at school?" Mother asked, smiling.

"It wasn't funny! I don't think I'll ever forget to put them in the wash again," Kenton declared.

"Your model car already got you side-tracked once again. Tell me what happened at school," Mother prompted.

"Well, Shana sits right across the aisle from me," Kenton explained slowly. "I guess girls have more sensitive noses, because Shana sat with a Kleenex over her nose. Boys sit in front and in back of me, but they didn't do that! Finally the teacher asked Shana if she had a bloody nose or a cold. Shana said something smelled bad. Then the teacher asked *me* if I knew what smelled bad. Oh, Mother, it was so embarrassing. At least Shana didn't say it smelled like dirty socks."

"But when your teacher asked what smelled, I am afraid she knew it was you. This is not only embarrassing to you, but to me also. Your teacher probably wonders what kind of a mother I am to let my boy come to school with smelly socks."

Iron sharpeneth iron; so a man sharpeneth the countenance of his friend.
Proverbs 27:17

"Oh, Mother, it's not your fault!" Kenton exclaimed. "Just yesterday morning you reminded me many times to get my dirty socks, but I didn't do it. So it is my fault that I went to school with dirty socks, not yours."

"But your teacher knows none of those facts," Mother pointed out. "So often when we do something wrong or forget to do something, it leaves a bad reflection on another person. I think you can call your teacher and Shana true friends. There's a verse in Proverbs that says, 'Faithful are the wounds of a friend.' If their words wounded you enough to cause you to be more mindful of putting your dirty socks in the wash, they have proven themselves to be friends," Mother said. "They both could have said, 'Kenton, your socks stink, but they didn't.' " She gave Kenton an encouraging smile.

"If you would remember, 'Action is the key. Do it immediately,' and put your dirty socks in the hamper right after you take them from your feet, your problem would be solved."

That evening when Kenton got ready for bed, he pulled off his socks and tossed them under his bed. Then suddenly he remembered. Getting down on his hands and knees, he began pulling socks out from under his bed. He picked up the pile and put them in his clothes hamper. Then he got down on his knees again and pulled out the socks under his desk and under his dresser, and then he put that pile in the hamper. Next he checked all his shoes and got out dirty socks and put them in the hamper. Now all his dirty socks were in the hamper.

But what was he going to wear to school tomorrow? He picked out a pair of socks and carried them to the bathroom. He ran water over the socks, then rubbed them with soap.

He scrubbed and rinsed them, squeezed out the extra water and hung them to dry on the shower curtain rod. Tomorrow he would have a clean pair of socks to wear to school and his mother would wash his socks in the hamper.

I think I have learned my lesson! Please God, help me to remember, "Action is the key. Do it immediately!"

"But Mother, I won't drop it!"

True story

"Mother, remember you said we can go to Horner's bakery and make a Mother's Day cake for Grandma? When are we going? Can we go today?" Lyndon asked in an excited voice.

"Tomorrow is the day, Lyndon. Tomorrow we can go to the market and decorate the cake," Mother explained for the sixth time.

"But Mother, I think you told me 'tomorrow,' yesterday."

"Well, I think you remember wrong," Mother replied. "The store will not have the cakes or decorations ready until tomorrow—just before Mother's Day. Now, why don't you go and pull some weeds from the blueberries? Danae is out in the garden already. If you keep busy, the time will pass more quickly."

"But Mother, I'd rather run the mower and mow the grass," Lyndon said.

"Not right now. I'm in the middle of making a casserole. I will come out later and help you do some mowing," Mother said.

"But Mother, I don't need your help mowing," Lyndon replied. "Harvey does their mowing all the time. I know how to mow."

"Lyndon, you have said, 'But Mother' three times. You are not listening to me—you are arguing with me—and that must stop! Harvey has a small lawn to mow with no flower gardens or baby trees," Mother explained. "We have twenty baby trees planted along the fence, and we certainly do not want them mowed down."

> When pride cometh, then cometh shame: but with the lowly is wisdom.
> Proverbs 11:2

"Oh, Mother, I would never try to mow down the new trees. I would be very careful," Lyndon promised.

"Yes, I know you would try to be careful, but you can get distracted very easily. I do not want you to mow until I can come outside," Mother said with finality.

Lyndon turned and silently went out the door. Mother finished making the casserole and put it into the oven. As she began cleaning up the kitchen, she heard the mower running. *I wonder if Danae finished in the garden and is starting to mow,* Mother thought. Then another thought came to her mind. *I wonder if Lyndon is running the mower.*

Mother hurried outside. Sure enough, Lyndon was running the mower. When Lyndon saw her coming, he shut off the mower.

"Why are you running the mower?" Mother asked. "You are supposed to be pulling weeds in the blueberry patch."

Sometimes Mirrors Lie

"I pulled some weeds and then I thought I would surprise you and get the mowing done," Lyndon explained, not looking up at his mother.

"Lyndon, look at me. What was the last thing I said to you before you went out the door?"

"Something . . . like . . . don't mow till you come. But I wanted to prove to you that I can mow without you. And see all I have mowed," Lyndon said as he pointed around the yard.

"But you disobeyed me; and what about the baby trees and the flower bed?" Mother asked, walking toward the row of little trees. She walked along the fence row and counted the trees—fifteen. "Why Lyndon, you mowed off five of the trees!"

"Did I really? I saw a rabbit running out in the field and the mower must've gone out of line," Lyndon explained. "That dumb rabbit caused me to go crooked! But I was very careful to stay away from your flower garden," he said, hoping that would pacify his mother.

"When your father comes home, you will explain to him what you did. You not only disobeyed me, but you mowed down five baby trees and then blamed it on the poor, innocent rabbit. And now you can put the mower away," Mother said, turning toward the house.

"But Mother, I am not finished mowing. Plea-s-"

"You are arguing again, Lyndon. You heard what I said."

When Dad came home, Lyndon explained to him what had happened.

"Well, Lyndon," Dad said, "you argued with Mother, you disobeyed, and you mowed down five new trees and did not take responsibility for what you did." Dad paused to let his words sink in.

"Son, you have too much self-confidence and pay too little attention to what you are told. You will need to go to your room and go to bed without supper," Dad continued. "I want you to do some serious thinking about your behavior. Talk to God about what happened today, Lyndon. He will help you, if you will ask Him. And this punishment can help you to remember to listen to instructions and to be obedient."

> A wise man will hear, and will increase learning; and a man of understanding shall attain unto wise counsels. Proverbs 1:5

The next morning a sober boy followed his parents to the car. They were going to Horner's Grocery. Some of his excitement over the Mother's Day cake had faded since last night's experience. Mother and Lyndon got out of the car and went into the store while Dad went to park the car.

The store had set up tables near the bakery, and other children were there decorating cakes. Mother picked out a cake and paid for it. Lyndon's enthusiasm came back as he scattered brightly colored sprinkles over the top of the cake. Then he chose a plastic cake topper pick which said, *Happy Mother's Day,* and placed it in the center of the cake. Mother placed the cake onto a tray and snapped on the plastic dome cover.

"Please, Mom, let me carry it," Lyndon begged. "It's my cake for Grandma."

"Okay," Mother said, "but be very careful not to drop it."

"Oh, I won't drop it!" Lyndon declared.

Mother and Lyndon stood outside the store and waited for Dad to come pick them up. They waited and waited; Dad was probably reading the newspaper while waiting in the car. Lyndon wiggled and squirmed. Again Mom warned him, "Don't drop the cake!"

Lyndon declared, "I won't drop it. I can handle it!"

Suddenly the car came into sight. "There comes Dad!" Lyndon exclaimed, motioning with his hands. In one wave and one jolt the cake landed on the sidewalk! Lyndon stared down in dismay.

"But Mother, I won't drop it!"

"Lyndon!" Mother exclaimed as she reached down to rescue the cake. Thankfully it appeared to have only a little crack from the sudden jolt.

A subdued boy climbed into the car, while Mother held the cake box. They were nearly home when he spoke up. "You know, Mother, if I wouldn't have been so sure of myself, I think I would have been more careful. The same thing with the mower—I really was proud that I could run the mower, but I got distracted and mowed over the baby trees and didn't even know it."

Lyndon was silent for a while and then added, "And when I am proud and confident of myself, I think I know more than you and I argue with you. I am really sorry, Mother. Will you forgive me? I am going to try to do better."

"Of course, I forgive you, Lyndon. Remember, self-confidence and pride take away precaution. Self-confidence causes you to close your ears to learning, listening, and obedience."

"I'm sorry I dropped the cake," Lyndon said seriously. "But I am glad I have learned a big lesson."

"And I think Grandma will still like the cake even if it has a crack in it," Mother assured him.

Sometimes Mirrors Lie

Too Rich to Sleep

True story

Juan climbed out of his truck, picked up his tools, and walked slowly to the worksite. He had been working for months on this rental house for his boss. The house really didn't need a remodel; it was nice—nicer than any house Juan had ever lived in. Nicer than any house he could ever hope to live in.

Today the boss was coming to look at the new flooring. What would Earl say? Juan could feel tension building in his mind. It seemed Earl was never satisfied with anything.

I think I'll put up the light fixtures first, he decided. He had three new fixtures installed when Earl walked in.

Earl walked through the house and came back into the kitchen. "Say, Juan, that color in the bathroom has to be changed. We don't like the shade. My wife and I went to the hardware last night and picked up new paint."

"Oh." That was all Juan could say.

"And this kitchen flooring, we decided we don't like it. You can come along with me this afternoon to Homebuilders and help me pick out new flooring," Earl said nonchalantly, as if pulling up new flooring and replacing it were an everyday occurrence.

"But Earl, you and your wife don't live here; you just rent this place out. Does it really matter that much?" Juan tried to reason with his boss. "That's going to be a lot of extra work and a lot of extra expense."

"That's not your problem. I pay you for your work," Earl stated as he headed toward the door. "I'll take my wife with me and you can stay here and start pulling up the flooring," he called over his shoulder.

"Oh well, I guess it's his money," Juan said to the four walls. "But why does that man constantly change his mind? It took two extra weeks to change the cupboards. And it took an extra week to move the island. And now I have to take up the flooring. I'll never get this job finished. It seems the more a person has, the more he wants and the less satisfied he is."

The following morning Earl and his wife were at the house when Juan came to work.

"The flooring and paint are here," Earl said. "I had Rob carry them in. And these light fixtures, I don't like them. I'm going to get some different ones."

"But I just . . ." Juan began.

Earl held up his hand and his wife spoke up. "You'd better

keep quiet. Earl hasn't had much sleep and his nerves are ready to snap."

"No, I haven't slept since 2 o'clock this morning—as usual," Earl stated.

"Oh, I'm so sorry. Are you feeling sick?" Juan asked.

"Sick? No. Fearful? Yes," Earl said. "I'm afraid someone might rob one of the houses or my shop or barn. Almost every night I hear strange noises, so I have to get up and drive around and check all the places for intruders. I can't sleep!"

"You poor man!" Juan exclaimed.

"No! I'm not poor. I'm rich—but I can't sleep," Earl stated.

"I guess you are like the rich man in the Bible who couldn't sleep because of his riches," Juan said.

> The sleep of a labouring man is sweet, whether he eat little or much: but the abundance of the rich will not suffer him to sleep. Ecclesiastes 5:12

"You believe the Bible?" Earl asked incredulously. Then, changing the subject, he commanded, "Be sure you get those new fixtures put up. This job has to be done by April 5."

Juan shook his head and sighed as they left. It must be terrible to have so much money that one couldn't sleep; he just couldn't comprehend it. *If he didn't have so much, maybe he would learn to be satisfied with things as they are. I don't know how I will ever get finished with this job if he keeps making changes.*

Juan worked hard day after day, but it seemed he was just spinning his wheels. He had never seen so much waste of time and money and building supplies. New light fixtures were piled in the corner of the dining room—fixtures that had been put up and taken down without even being used.

Several days later Earl walked into the bathroom where Juan was painting. "I want you to go out and help Rob and the other fellows move some bushes. Those blueberry bushes need to be moved to the other side of the drive."

"But Earl, I am painting and need . . ." Juan began.

"Forget it and go help the other fellows," Earl demanded. "And when you are finished with the blueberries, I want you to go to that rental house across the road and check the plumbing under the sink. There seems to be a leak somewhere."

"Yes, sir," Juan replied. *Well, there goes the day without finishing the painting in the bathroom. Money sure hasn't bought Earl peace, happiness, or contentment. His money is just a big burden to him—and his dissatisfaction is a distress to his workers.*

It was a week later—April 2—and Juan felt time was closing in on him. He had always worked hard and tried to please his employers. But he simply could not please Earl. He was working hard at changing the light fixtures, not for the second time, but for the third time, when Earl walked in with a roar.

"You are not going to get this job finished on time!" he accused. "Shall I fire you or will you just quit?"

"I will finish what I'm working on now and I will give you my answer this evening," Juan said quietly. He felt sorry for Earl, but for his own peace of mind, he knew it was time to move on.

Learn to Listen—
Listen to Learn

True story

The morning sun shone through the dining room window, and a cool Oregon breeze rippled the curtains. "Maria and Anna," Mom said at the breakfast table, "I would like you to do some weeding in the garden this morning while it's nice. And you, Luis, should do your chicken chores and take care of the rabbits."

"Oh, Mom, it is too cold this morning," Maria complained.

"In a very short time you will be complaining that it is too hot," Mom said. "I want you to go out now. I will clean up the kitchen and soon be out to help you."

The children headed out the door and Mom proceeded to clean up the kitchen. As she crossed the yard to the garden, she could not see anyone working between the rows of vegetables. Then she heard a banging sound. She hurried toward

A wise man will hear, and will increase learning; and a man of understanding shall attain unto wise counsels: Proverbs 1:5

the source of the noise. There were the children, holding sticks and gathered around the propane tank, enjoying the hollow sounding music the sticks made on the side of the tank.

"What are you doing out here?" Mom asked. "Have you all forgotten what I told you about not playing near the propane tank? This is not the place to play; besides, you each had a job to do and you are not obeying. Now, girls, come to the garden, and Luis, you go to the barn and finish your chores."

The girls worked faithfully with Mom by their side. Garden work always went better when Mom was there. The sun was getting warmer and the girls were getting hot, but they kept working.

Suddenly they heard a loud scream from Luis. Mom and the girls ran from the garden and around the corner of the house. There stood Luis by the propane tank, blood running down his face.

"I'm bleeding. I'm bleeding!" he screamed. "I'm going to die!"

"No, no, you'll be all right," Mom assured him. "Just calm down." She took her apron from around her waist, folded it, and pressed it to Luis's bleeding forehead. She held it tightly against his wound while Anna ran to the house to get a large bandage.

Mom put a temporary bandage over the cut and took Luis into the house. She cleaned out the cut with peroxide and carefully covered it with an antibiotic cream. It was a large cut and needed to be taped together. Then she put on a clean bandage. Holding up the mirror, Mom said to Luis, "Now look at yourself; that's the result of your disobedience."

"Will I have to wear this big bandage to school?" Luis asked.

"Yes, you will," Mom said. "Now tell me how you got the cut." Mom thought she knew what had happened but she wanted to hear it from Luis.

"I-I—climbed up on the propane tank," he said. "I was just trying to use the tank for a slide and—and I fell off."

"Were you supposed to be on the propane tank?" Mom asked. "Were you obeying me?"

"No. I'm sorry I disobeyed. I guess the propane tank doesn't make a very good slide; it is too far to the ground," Luis said as a tear trickled down his cheek. "My head hurts."

"You go to your bed and lie down. No reading and no playing with toys. Just rest until we come in from the garden."

> My son, hear the instruction of thy father, and forsake not the law of thy mother. Proverbs 1:8

o o o o o o o o o o o o o o

Two years had passed since the propane tank accident. "Luis, I heard that you were jumping from the swing while you were swinging really high. Is that true?" Mom asked one afternoon after school.

"So who told you? Maria's a tattle-tale," he concluded.

"It doesn't matter who told me," Mom said. "I asked you a question: Were you jumping from a high swing?"

"Yes, but why can't I, Mom? Everyone else does it. Why can't I have fun like the rest? I like to feel like I'm flying," Luis said with a grin.

"Luis, I have explained this to you before. Do you remember what I told you?" Mom asked, looking him in the eye. Luis shrugged and looked down at the floor.

"Sit down here at the table and look at me," Mom instructed. "Luis, your bones are not strong like other children's. As a baby and toddler you did not have good nourishment. Because your family was poor, you did not get enough good food and vitamins to make strong bones. Before your mom died in Guatemala she fed you as well as she could, but when we adopted you, your bones were not strong because of malnutrition."

"Pull up your pant legs a little and look at your legs and ankles."

Luis slowly reached down and pulled up one pant leg.

"Now look at your wrists and arms," Mom said. "What do you see?"

"They look skinny," Luis said. "But I am stronger than I look," he insisted.

"It isn't your fault that they look that way, son. But you are responsible to take care of the body God has given you. I am telling you for the last time. Don't jump from the swings while swinging high. We don't want any broken bones."

"Yes, Mom," Luis replied with a sigh.

Sometimes Mirrors Lie

For several days Luis stopped jumping from the swings. Then the other boys began calling him a sissy. He couldn't stand that. *I'm eating good food now; I'm getting stronger,* he reasoned. But when he looked at his legs and arms, they still looked skinny compared to the other boys.

Finally he told himself, *I'm tired of being called a sissy. I'm not a baby anymore. I'll show those boys at school how daring I am!*

The next day at school Luis jumped onto the swing. He pumped higher and higher. The wind swooshed through his hair and he felt as though he could fly. When the swing reached the top, he jumped.

Flying through the air was fun—but the hard landing was

not. Luis lay on the ground, screaming in pain while his friends looked on helplessly. "Oh, look at his arm!" someone exclaimed. "Run and get the teacher."

Luis looked at his crooked arm as torrents of tears ran down his face. How his arm hurt! He had never before felt such pain. His once straight arm had a curve like the pipe elbow that fits under the sink.

Luis's mom was called and she came to school and drove Luis to the closest emergency room. At the hospital the x-rays showed both bones broken in his lower arm and very nearly puncturing the skin.

The doctor put Luis's arm in a plaster cast from above the elbow down to his hand. Only his thumb and fingers stuck out, and they were difficult to use because of the position they were in.

"No more jumping from a swing for you," the doctor said. "This cast should be a good reminder for several weeks."

Luis grinned and nodded.

The next weeks in school were difficult. Luis had to learn to write with his left hand. For a while he could not run and play with the other children for fear of falling. Through those difficult days and weeks of pain, Luis often wished he had listened to his mom's warning. He told himself, *I didn't listen and learn, but now I have learned to listen the hard way. From now on I will pay more attention to what Mom tells me.*

Sometimes Mirrors Lie

Moonlight, Dream Come True

Shawn wanted a pony. For years he had wanted a pony, but Dad always said there wasn't enough money for ponies, not even for one. Finally Shawn decided to turn one of the milk cows into a "horse." He would catch this cow with a crooked nose and ride her in from the pasture in the evening.

Shawn named his pretend pony Crook. He would go out into the pasture and call, "Come, Crook. Come, Crook." When the cow saw or heard Shawn, she would turn and run the other way. Shawn never did figure out whether she disliked her name or disliked the ride.

When Shawn finally caught the cow and got on her, she would placidly walk along bearing her burden. Sometimes Shawn stood on her back as she walked calmly toward the barn. It didn't feel like much of a horseback ride but this cow-horse would have to do for now, he decided.

One day Shawn's friend Nelson came to visit. "We have a pony we want to sell," Nelson told him with a laugh. "If you get a pony you won't have to ride your dad's cow."

Sometimes Mirrors Lie

"I'd love to buy your pony, but we don't have the money," Shawn replied.

"Why don't you get some extra jobs and earn the money yourself?" Nelson suggested.

"Say, that's a great idea," Shawn answered. "I'll ask my dad and get back to you,"

That evening at the supper table, Shawn brought up the idea of a pony and him working for the money.

"Well, that sounds like a good idea—if you don't neglect your work here at home for your moneymaking jobs," Dad replied. "But remember, a pony will take food also."

"I'll earn enough money to pay for the pony—and then I'll have to keep some of my jobs to pay for the food, I guess," Shawn said. "But I think I can do it."

The very next morning Shawn walked to Nelson's house. "I'm going to work all summer to earn the $175 for the pony," he told his friend. Nelson promised that they would save the pony for him.

That very afternoon Shawn went to the neighbors and got a lawn-mowing job. He painted a fence for another neighbor. Then he found another lawn-mowing job. He pulled weeds from an older lady's flower garden and burned her trash. And so it went from one job to another, and always he stashed the money away to pay for the pony.

One evening Shawn counted his savings, stored in an old

Pride goeth before destruction, and an haughty spirit before a fall.
Proverbs 16:18

birthday card box in the corner of his dresser drawer. He had $115 so far. Hmm . . . That could buy a pretty nice bike and he wouldn't have to feed it! *No, I'd rather have a pony,* Shawn decided. He put his money back into the box. He would work some more.

By the end of summer Shawn had the $175 to give to Nelson.

How pleased Shawn was. He had his own pony and he had worked hard to pay for it. It was a Welsh pony about four-and-a-half feet tall at the shoulders. Because of the pony's color and markings, Shawn named him Moonlight. He had a moon-shape on both sides of his shoulders, surrounded by a nice white band. He was tan with a white mane and tail. Moonlight was beautiful—a dream come true.

"May I ride your pony?" his brother Brent asked. "I sure wish we had a saddle."

"Ah—you don't need one," Shawn said. "Just wrap your legs around the pony and hang on tight. I never wish for a saddle," he boasted.

Shawn knew the pony sometimes bucked. Moonlight had tried to get him off his back several times, but Shawn was short and could wrap his legs around the pony's belly.

Brent was tall and his legs were longer. He had a hard time wrapping them around the pony tight enough to stay on, but he tried—and off they went. But suddenly the pony bucked and Brent went flying off the pony. Moonlight trotted off, freed from his burden.

Brent tried another ride on Moonlight, but again ended up on the ground. After several more tries, he gave up. "That pony is crazy! Why does he think he has to buck someone off all the time?"

"Oh, he's easy to ride. He never bucked me off. You just don't hang on tight enough," Shawn said with a laugh. "Watch me!" Off he galloped down the lane and out into the field. Several times Moonlight bucked, but his burden stayed on his back.

"One of these times, brother, he's going to buck you off," Brent remarked as Shawn came riding back.

When pride cometh, then cometh shame: but with the lowly is wisdom.
Proverbs 11:2

Shawn rode proudly up and down the lane. Again Moonlight tried to buck him off. Shawn ended up with his legs wrapped tightly around the pony's neck, one hand hanging on to the horse's mane, and the other hand pulling hard on the rein. Moonlight turned circles with Shawn hanging onto his neck, until he decided it was no use to try to get rid of his rider. Then Shawn pulled himself up onto the horse's back again and off they would ride.

One day the heifers got out and started running down the road. Shawn knew he would need Moonlight to help him get them back in. Shawn ran to the stall and quickly grabbed the bridle and put it on Moonlight. He jumped onto the pony's back and took off toward the road. Shawn expected Moonlight to run after the loose heifers, but instead, the pony immediately turned and bucked. Moonlight did not want to chase heifers.

"Oh—o-o-oh," Shawn groaned as he flew over the pony's head and landed on the road with a thud. Moonlight ran back to the barn and Shawn ran after him, frustrated and angry. As Shawn ran, he thought of the times he had bragged about never being dumped from Moonlight's back. He couldn't say that anymore!

Shawn jumped back on Moonlight and directed him toward the heifers. The heifers were soon rounded up, safely off the road, and back in their pen. But Shawn was steaming from both exertion and frustration.

Why am I so angry? Shawn wondered. *If I wouldn't have been so proud about Moonlight not being able to buck me off, this probably wouldn't even bother me.*

Shawn put Moonlight back into the stall, and stood with his arms resting on the top boards, thinking. A light turned on in his mind. He had often heard that pride brings shame, but now he understood what that meant. Slowly his anger melted away, replaced by humility.

Now that he had let go of his pride, maybe he could work at training Moonlight not to buck.

Sometimes Mirrors Lie

Eddie and the Bike

Based on a true incident

"Look, Mother, I'm doing it!" Eddie yelled as he rode down the driveway on his new two-wheeler bike. Just yesterday he had started with training wheels but he no longer needed them.

Sometimes, though, he began to wobble and had to put his foot down to keep from falling. He didn't want to crash his bike. With its shiny red paint and silver trim it still looked brand new.

"That's good," Mother said from the front porch. "You're getting better all the time."

Eddie turned the bike around at the end of the drive. This time he was half-way to the house before he began to tip. He hopped off before he fell. Soon he would be riding without tipping at all.

"Dinner's almost ready," Mother said as she turned to go back into the house. "It's time to put your bike in the garage and come in and get washed."

Eddie knew he should obey right now—but he wanted to ride down the driveway just once more. He hopped back on the bike and began pedaling, hardly wobbling at all. It was such fun! But suddenly he was going fast and getting too near the street. He put on the brakes and turned the handlebars to keep from tipping. The bike rolled off the driveway, across the lawn, and smack into the neighbors' flower garden. Eddie fell off the bike and landed in a rosebush as his bike flopped over into a bed of lilies.

Eddie scrambled to his feet and rubbed his hand. It hurt where a thorn had poked it. He felt like crying. He picked up his bike and looked it over. No scratches. No bent wheels. There were some leaves sticking to it from the plants it had landed on but otherwise it seemed to be all right. He breathed a sigh of relief.

Then Eddie saw the lilies—four beautiful pink lilies had broken stems. Their neighbors, Mr. and Mrs. Johnson, loved flowers and worked in their flower garden every day. Eddie was sorry he'd broken the lilies. How he wished he had put his bike away when his mother told him to! He should have obeyed.

Would the Johnsons be angry at him for ruining their flowers? But maybe no one would notice. He certainly hoped so.

He tried to straighten the broken lilies but it was no use. They wouldn't stand up again. He pulled some grass from the lawn and tossed it over the flowers. They were partly hidden.

Sometimes Mirrors Lie

Then he pulled some more grass. It didn't look as bad as before.

He turned the bike back into his driveway and walked to the garage to put it away, then hurried into the kitchen to wash for dinner.

"You're awfully quiet, Eddie," Father said at dinner. "How are you doing with the new bike?"

Eddie didn't feel like talking. Those broken lilies seemed to be staring him in the face and he felt terrible. Even if Mother and Father didn't find out, Jesus knew. "I'm doing all right, but I need to practice more," he said.

He that covereth his sins shall not prosper: but whoso confesseth and forsaketh them shall have mercy.

Proverbs 28:13

He didn't want his parents to know what had happened, but he was sure Jesus would want him to tell. He took a spoonful of mashed potatoes, but it was hard to swallow.

"I did something bad," he said.

"What did you do?" Mother asked.

"I didn't stop riding my bike when you told me to," Eddie said. "I-I wanted to take just one more ride down the driveway and I got going too fast. I put on the brakes and turned, b-but I crashed into the Johnsons' garden and broke off some of their flowers."

"That is too bad. You know you should have minded Mother. What do you think you should do now?" Father asked.

Eddie felt a tear running down his cheek. "I don't know. I can't fix the flowers. They are all broken and on the ground."

"No," said Father. "You certainly can't fix them. Can you

think of something else?"

Eddie had almost five dollars in his piggy bank. "Maybe we could go to the store and I could buy some other flowers for Mr. and Mrs. Johnson. How much do lilies cost?"

"I don't think that would be the same for them," Mother said. "They planted those lilies and they bloom every summer. The ones you buy would be already picked and would last only a few days."

Now Eddie felt really sorry. Was there no way to make things right? Was Jesus disappointed in him?

"Perhaps we could go over to the Johnson's house after dinner and you could tell them you're sorry and you didn't mean to do it," Father said. "Would you like to do that?"

Eddie swallowed hard. "I guess," he murmured.

After dinner Eddie and Father walked over to their neighbors. They showed Mr. and Mrs. Johnson the broken lilies. "I'm sorry," Eddie said. "I crashed my bike. I didn't mean to do it."

> Even a child is known by his doings, whether his work be pure, and whether it be right. Proverbs 20:11

Mr. Johnson examined the broken lilies. "These are my favorites—Stargazers," he said. "The grass doesn't really hide them very well. Makes me think of the verse in Numbers that says, 'Be sure your sin will find you out,' " he said. He patted Eddie on the head. "The lilies will grow again next year. Thank you for telling me what happened. I am glad you want to be an honest boy. I know you didn't do it on purpose." He lifted several of the broken stems and pinched them off. He handed the pink blooms to Eddie. "Why don't you give these to your mother?"

When Eddie and Father returned home, Eddie ran to Mother. He handed her the lilies and gave her a hug. "I really wish I would have quit riding when you called. Then I wouldn't have crashed into the flowers."

Mother lifted the flowers to her face. "M-m-m, they smell so good." She took Eddie's scratched hand in hers and kissed it. "I'm sorry you were hurt, but doing wrong always hurts ourselves and often hurts others," she said. "I know you didn't mean to hurt the flowers. We all make mistakes, but the important thing is that we learn from our mistakes and don't make them again. It was nice of Mr. Johnson to give them to us. They can be a reminder for the next few days."

Eddie felt like a load had been lifted. He broke into a smile.

That night when Eddie knelt by his bed to pray, he said, "Thank you, Jesus, that Mr. Johnson was so nice to me and did not get angry. Help me to be more careful from now on."

—Marie Latta

Tammy's Birthday Sweater

True story

"Mom! Look! My birthday box from Grandma." Tammy burst into the house carrying a big package.

Grandma always gave her something special for her birthday. Last year she had sent the book *Little Women* and a beautiful pair of knitted socks. Tammy wore the socks whenever she went ice skating. They were so nice and warm. Two years ago Grandma had sent a lovely dresser set of crocheted doilies she had made especially to match Tammy's bedroom. What had she sent this year?

Tammy tore open the box and found a wrapped package inside. Grandma had used white shelf paper and had written "Happy Birthday, Tammy" again and again with different colored pens. In place of a bow, Grandma had glued on a sunburst of gold ribbons.

It's almost too pretty to open, Tammy thought, but she carefully removed the paper and lifted the cover of the box. Inside were two sweaters, one powder blue and the other soft lavender. Tammy held the blue sweater up to her cheek. It felt so soft and warm. Then she did the same with the lavender one. It was just as soft and warm as the other. She didn't know which one she liked best.

Sometimes Mirrors Lie

"I can't wait to wear these to church and school, Mom," Tammy said. "Grandma must have spent a lot of time knitting these. The only problem is, I don't know which one to wear first." She laughed.

Mom had been peeling carrots, but now she dried her hands on a kitchen towel and held the lavender sweater up in front of Tammy. "You'll look nice in the blue one, but I like the lavender on you too. You'll just have to decide. You can't wear both of them at once! Right now, though, wouldn't you like to call Grandma and thank her?"

Tammy nodded. She wished Grandma lived closer so she could see her and give her a big hug. She called Grandma's number and could almost see Grandma smiling as they talked. "I enjoyed making the sweaters for you, honey," Grandma said. "You know how I like to knit."

Tammy had just gotten off the phone when there was a knock at the door. "I'll get it, Mom," she said.

Mr. Gordon, their neighbor from the farm down the road, stood on the porch. After Tammy asked him to come in, her mother pulled out a chair at the table for him and sat down to talk.

"Did you hear about the Masons' house over on Twenty Mile Road? It burned down last night," Mr. Gordon said.

"Oh, no, that's terrible! I'm sorry to hear it," Mom said. "Was anyone hurt?"

"No, they all got out safely and even saved their cat—but the house is a total loss . . . and everything in it," Mr. Gordon said. "They have only the clothes they were wearing. The family is staying with Mrs. Mason's parents for now."

Tammy's Birthday Sweater

"We'll certainly remember them in our prayers. What else can we do to help?" Mom asked.

"I'm taking up a collection from the neighbors," Mr. Gordon said. "As soon as the Masons can find a house to rent, they'll need furniture, appliances, dishes, and just about everything."

"What about clothes?" Tammy asked. Laurie Mason was her friend, and she'd been looking forward to showing her the new sweaters from Grandma. Now Laurie probably didn't have any sweaters at all.

"Mrs. Mason and her mother went to Goodwill this morning and got a few items of clothing," Mr. Gordon said. "But she lost her purse in the fire and the money that was in it too."

Tammy was thinking hard. *How would it feel to have your house burn and lose all your possessions? The Bible said to "do unto others as you would have them do unto you."* She really wanted to do something for Laurie and her family.

While Mom reached for her purse, Tammy picked up the blue sweater Grandma had sent. She handed it to Mr. Gordon. "Take this to Laurie," she said. "She's the same size as I am and I know she'll like it."

"Are you sure, Tammy?" her mother asked. "You have other sweaters in Laurie's size. You haven't even worn this one yet."

"I'm sure," Tammy said. She hoped Laurie would like it as much as she did.

"I'm pleased with your sacrifice, Tammy," Mom said. "That sweater is a lovely gift and I know you wanted to wear it. As it says in Proverbs, 'A friend loveth at all times.' You're living that verse."

Mr. Gordon nodded. "I'll wait—if you want to get another sweater in place of this new one."

"No," Tammy said. "I want Laurie to have this one."

That evening Tammy called her grandmother again to explain what she had done with one of her sweaters. "I'm so glad I made two of them," Grandma said. "It makes me happy to think of both of you girls wearing them, and I am so pleased that you shared with your friend."

> A friend loveth at all times, and a brother is born for adversity.
> Proverbs 17:17

The next day, while Tammy was setting the table for dinner, Mother called her to the phone. "It's Laurie Mason," she said.

"Hi, Laurie," Tammy said into the phone. "Mr. Gordon told us about your house burning. I'm so sorry, but I'm glad you all got out."

"Thanks, Tammy. It really was terrible—" Her voice caught but she went on bravely. "We're thankful no one was hurt. Dad says God was watching over us. But Tammy, I'm calling to thank you for the beautiful sweater. It's the nicest piece of clothing I have. I really like it!"

"Oh, Laurie, I'm so glad. My grandma sent two sweaters for my birthday and I wanted to share with you. Let's both wear our new sweaters to school on Monday, okay?"

"Wonderful! And guess what? One of the skirts my mom found for me at Goodwill is dark blue and will be perfect with the new blue sweater. I really appreciate your giving it to me. I'll remember this for a long time, Tammy. Thanks again."

Tammy hung up the phone. Even better than the feeling of wearing her new sweater was the happy feeling of sharing with a friend.

—Marie Latta

26

Under the Wings

True story

Sheila stuck her feet into her tan thongs and headed out the back door into the freshness of the warm springtime air. She tugged open the barn door, grabbed a bucket and filled it with chicken feed, then hurried to the chicken pen. The cackling hens gathered around her. The rooster stood on an empty box, stretched his neck, and let out a loud *Cock-a-doodle-doo!* Sheila enjoyed her time with the chickens on Saturday. During the week when she had to go to school, her older brother tended the chickens.

Sheila laughed when Henny Penny appeared with her six fluffy chicks, wanting breakfast for herself and the babies. Sheila spread a pile of feed for the big hens and then scattered more feed in another corner for Henny Penny and her babies. Now they could scratch and peck and get their share, away from the flock.

Sheila filled the feeder with the remainder of the grain from the pail. Then she walked to the center of the pen. She watched the hens fighting for bits and pieces of grain, and she admired the baby chicks. It amazed her how they knew to scratch and peck just like their mother.

Suddenly a moving shadow crossed the chicken pen. Sheila heard a cluck from Henny Penny, and the chicks disappeared. She looked up and saw a hawk circling. She waved her bucket at the hawk—and off he flew. Soon Henny Penny gave another call, which the chicks recognized as an "all clear." Out from under their mother's wings they scurried, to peck and scratch again.

Those chicks sure seem to know their lives depend on their obedience. It's amazing to see the intelligence, or instinct, that God gave the animals, Sheila thought. *And even most of the older hens ran for shelter. They just know a hawk isn't a friend.*

Hmm. I think the chickens have taught me a lesson today— maybe a couple of lessons. Prompt obedience is for my own good. And when I'm in trouble I have a shelter. Jesus is my shelter in the time of danger.

○ ○ ○ ○ ○ ○ ○ ○ ○ ○ ○ ○ ○ ○

Far away on a large chicken farm in another state, lived the Miller girls, Sandra and Sabrina. The Miller family owned thousands of chickens and gathered dozens and dozens of eggs.

While the Miller girls did the chicken chores, they kept an eye out for dead chickens. Some chickens died from sickness and others from being crippled and unable to get to the feed and water.

Sometimes Mirrors Lie

"Chickens sure don't seem to have much love for each other," Sabrina commented. "It is each for her own. If they'd have even an ounce of compassion they wouldn't just keep pecking and pecking on some unfortunate hen that got injured or something."

"Why do they do that?" Sandra wondered. "But I guess children sometimes do the same thing. Why does a group of children pick on one child?"

"I don't know about children," Sabrina replied, "but chickens can sure be mean when they spot a weak hen. They peck on her because she is either smaller than the rest or bleeding somewhere. They peck on her until a big spot is bare of feathers. This just makes the hen all the more obvious, and they peck at her some more. The hen-pecked chicken tries to hide, but sometimes they peck her until she dies."

> The name of the Lord is a strong tower: the righteous runneth into it, and is safe. Proverbs 18:10

"And that is why we have to find dead chickens and get them out of the hen house," Sandra replied with disgust. "If they cared more for each other, they would not be pecking all the time.

"And I have another thought," Sandra said. "If we humans cared more for each other, we wouldn't be picking at each other either."

"That is so true," Sabrina said. "And it even applies to us sisters!" She grinned at Sandra.

One day the girls found something that amazed them. It

was time to check the chicken nests for dead birds. Sabrina walked between the feed lines. Up on the slats the nests were about waist high. She had to bend down and then twist her neck sideways to look into the nests.

The job had a rhythm. Sabrina slid her left hand along the pipe, pushed the nest curtain back with the stick in her right hand, checked for dead chickens, took a few steps, and started over. Sabrina moved along quickly.

But when she pushed back the flap on one nest, Sabrina got a surprise.

What was she seeing?

A hen sat in the nest, with one wing stretched out. Was that a chicken tail sticking out from under her wing? Sure enough! A hen-pecked chicken with barely any feathers was snuggled under the wing of a motherly hen. Ah, so some chickens did care for others! Astounding!

"Sandra!" Sabina called, "come see what I found!" She poked her stick at the motherly hen—and was told in squawking hen language to stay away. The poor, almost featherless chicken nudged in farther under the sheltering wing. The girls could hardly believe what they were seeing.

"Isn't it amazing—the instinct God has given animals?" Sabrina asked as she finished her job. "She is not a mother hen protecting her young. She is a young chicken protecting another young chicken. It may have been her sister, her aunt, her cousin, or her friend—no matter. There was a job that needed to be done and this hen is doing it." She shook her head in amazement.

"It reminds me of God's protection," Sandra said. "It does not matter who you are—you are His child. God is always there when you run to Him."

"That doesn't mean we will never have painful things in life," Sabrina added. "We don't like to go through hard things, but often the hard things teach us how much we need God."

"When we are hurt and feel pecked on," Sandra went on, "we can hide under God's wing. He won't let any harm come to the child in His care."

"He wants to be a refuge for us, just as that motherly hen is to that hen-pecked chicken. He desires only the best for us, and He is a safe place to go with our troubles," Sabrina concluded.

—Sabrina Miller

So Easy for God

True stories

Part One: A Pair of Glasses

Judy and her sister Jean had been out in the garden digging potatoes. That was the after-school job Mom had assigned them on this damp fall day. It hadn't been pleasant to pick up the rough-skinned potatoes with stiff, cold fingers, but it was wonderful to know they had finally finished the last rows. Now buckets and buckets of potatoes were stored in the basement for use during the coming winter.

"I can hardly wait to see what Mom's making for supper," remarked Jean while she pulled off her scarf and coat. "I'm so-o hungry."

"So am I!" Judy said. She slid her hand into her coat pocket to pull out her glasses. Then she gasped in dismay. Nothing was there except a gaping hole in the bottom of her pocket.

"Oh," wailed Judy, "my glasses! They're gone! I took them off while we were digging potatoes because they were a nuisance to my nose and hurting my ears . . ."

"Look in your other pocket," suggested Jean. "You probably just forgot which one you put them in."

> The Lord is far from the wicked: but he heareth the prayer of the righteous.
> Proverbs 15:29

But nothing was in the other pocket either. "I guess I'll have to go look in the garden," Judy said. She trudged up the basement steps, a sinking feeling in her heart.

The glasses were a new pair, the first ones she'd ever had, and she knew they were expensive. Mom and Dad would be so disappointed when they heard she'd lost them.

Judy hurried across the lawn now, nearing the garden. "Dear God," she prayed, "please help me find my glasses. They cost my dad and mom a lot of money and I don't want them to have to buy another pair. I need glasses to read better too. So if it's your will, show me where they are. In Jesus' name, Amen."

Carefully Judy picked her way up and down the ridges of dirt where she and Jean had been digging potatoes. Would she ever find her glasses, or were they buried in the loose dirt somewhere? Maybe they'd turn up in pieces when Dad plowed the garden later in the fall.

Her thoughts were growing as gloomy as the weather and she was nearly ready to give up searching. *But God knows where they are,* she mused, *and wouldn't it be easy for Him to show them to me?* And then she saw it—a bit of hard smooth plastic peeking out of the dirt.

"My glasses!" she cried. She snatched them up, still folded, and breathed a sigh of relief. The lenses were caked with garden soil, but nothing was broken or even scratched.

"Thank you, God," she whispered. "You do care and you do answer prayer!" Then she ran to the house to clean up her glasses and to tell Mom the good news.

o o o o o o o o o o o o o o

Part Two: Blondie, the Jersey Cow

The Larson family had what they called an "Old McDonald's Farm," with a "quack, quack" here and a "moo, moo" there, and a "cluck, cluck" everywhere. A few chickens supplied the family with eggs, and once in a while they enjoyed duck eggs. Blondie, their Jersey cow, supplied them with lots of milk and cream, which could be turned into butter, cottage cheese, yogurt, and even ice cream.

One morning, Dan came running into the house, "Daddy! Daddy, Blondie won't get up. She is acting very sick."

Dad took his son's hand. "Well, let's go out and see what is wrong."

Laura called out from the chicken pen when she saw her dad. "I got eight eggs this morning, Dad, and there is one sick chicken in here."

"I'll have to check on the chicken later," Dad called back.

Dad and Dan stood looking at Blondie. "Yes, she is very sick. I expect she has mastitis—and I don't have enough money to call the vet out. They charge so much to come way out here and we can't haul her in to him."

"What is mastitis?" Dan asked. "Will she die?"

"She has an infection in her udder." Dad crawled over the fence and knelt beside their gentle milk cow. He spoke softly to her as he felt her udder. "She is very sick. Her udder is swollen and hot."

"Dan, run to the house and tell Mother and the other children to come out here. "

Dan turned and hurried to the house. Why would Dad want the rest of the family to come out? He gave Mom the message and soon they were all out in the pasture.

Dad stayed by Blondie with one hand on her side. "Come, Mother, let's pray. Do you all believe that God can heal her?" he asked.

"Yes," everyone replied.

Then they bowed their heads and Dad prayed that God would heal their milk cow, if it was His will.

They all let out a sigh at the end of the prayer. Now they would wait to see what God would do.

"Mother, could you fill a pail in the kitchen with some warm water? Dan can bring it out here to the cow. I have to leave for work. You children can keep an eye on Blondie and keep praying for her."

Sometimes Mirrors Lie

When Dad arrived home that evening an excited bunch of children was waiting for him.

"Blondie got up!"

"Blondie is getting better!"

"Blondie ate a little! God is answering our prayer!" Dad was greeted with exclamations on all sides.

"Oh, praise the Lord!" Dad responded. "God is healing our wonderful milk cow so we can keep her."

So Easy for God

Yesenia's Song

As told by a missionary

Yesenia carefully scrubbed the dried mud from her white shoes, then she put them into the sunshine to dry. A white dress was draped over a shrub, also drying in the bright rays. She had washed the dress by hand and now she carried it into the house and carefully hung it up. She wanted to look her very best for the Christmas program tonight.

Yesenia was the only person in her family who went to church. Natalie, the pastor's daughter, had invited her one Sunday, and since then she rarely missed a service. The children who attended church had been practicing for a Christmas program. Christmas was only three days away.

"Please, Mama, you will go with me to the Christmas program tonight? You will come to hear me sing?" Yesenia asked with bright, shining eyes.

"Yes, I will come," Yesenia's mother agreed.

"Bueno! Bueno!" [1] Yesenia said, hopping up and down. She wanted her mother to hear the special solo she had been assigned. "Glory to God in the highest, and on earth, peace, good will to man," she would sing. It was the chorus of the angels, so she was going to dress in white.

Yesenia and her mother, along with some neighbors, climbed onto the back of the pickup truck that was waiting for them. They carried umbrellas because dark, threatening clouds were rolling in from the south.

The truck made a few more stops and soon it was packed full. A few raindrops started to fall. Yesenia's mother opened a big umbrella and held it high over their heads—just in time. A heavy downpour pelted the umbrellas—and the heads of those who were not protected.

The neighbors and friends shouted good-naturedly over the din. Everyone was in good spirits, though the rain was cold. Yesenia and Natalie bent their heads together and sang the first verse of "*Noche de Paz,*" [2] for extra practice. Yesenia shivered and pulled her towel around her shoulders a little closer and stood tightly against Natalie.

When the truck had eased into the church parking lot and come to a stop, Yesenia gingerly stepped out over the tailgate onto the muddy bumper and hopped carefully to the ground.

---

[1] "Good! Good!"

[2] "Silent Night," literally, "Night of Peace."

Sometimes Mirrors Lie

She tried to keep her shoes and dress clean, but it was impossible. She went to the faucet near the outdoor bathrooms to rinse off some mud that had splattered onto her dress. Her mother waited for her, holding the umbrella, and then they walked into the cement block building together.

The children sang with enthusiasm. Yesenia was nervous when she sang her solo, but she did her best. Her sweet voice lifted in the praise chorus of the angels. She even looked like an angel dressed in white, some said. As she finished the song, she imagined the shining angels with shimmering robes and soft wings, praising God that night long ago on the hills of Bethlehem.

The pastor shared the Christmas story, how Jesus was born in a stable and the shepherds who came to visit Him there. Then he told about the wise men who followed the star and later found Jesus in a house with His parents. He told of Jesus growing to be a man who went about doing good, healing the sick, giving sight to the blind, and even raising the dead. Then he shared the good news of Jesus' death for the sins of the world and the hope that His death offers to all people. "Today, Jesus is in heaven preparing a beautiful place for those who believe in Him and obey Him," the pastor said. "Jesus is waiting with open arms for each of us, and we can go to live with Him if we love and obey Him while we are here on earth."

Yesenia had heard the story many times, but she never grew

In the transgression of an evil man there is a snare: but the righteous doth sing and rejoice.

Proverbs 29:6

tired of hearing about Jesus. *When I grow up, I am going to be a Christian,* she thought.

When Yesenia and Mama entered their little cement house that evening, Papa was sitting at the table, reading a newspaper by the light of a kerosene lamp. He smiled at them.

Yesenia kissed his cheek. "Hello, Papa. Did you have a good day of work on the *loma?*"[3]

"Yes, except for the rain on the way home. The mule struggled to stay on his feet on the way down," Papa answered.

Yesenia's mother set plates of boiled green bananas on the table. She used a match to light the gas stove and fried some eggs in hot oil. She put an egg over the bananas on Yesenia's plate and poured some oil over it. She put two eggs on Papa's plate. Then they took their plates and began to eat. Mama brought them each a tin cup of water.

Yesenia was tired when she crawled under the mosquito net into her little bed. She closed her eyes. Images of shepherds, a baby in a manger, wise men, and angels replayed themselves in her mind until she fell asleep.

She dreamed she was in a beautiful place with bright flowers, a sparkling river, and many children dressed in white. She heard lovely music in the distance and curiously wandered toward it. She heard a great chorus of angels singing in perfect harmony: "Glory to God in the highest, peace on earth, good will to man."

Then someone walked toward her with His arms open wide,

---

[3] *Loma* refers to farmland on a mountainside.

Sometimes Mirrors Lie

welcoming her to join the song. She knew it was Jesus! She stood with the angels, her voice blending perfectly with theirs. She felt happier and more at home than she had ever felt anywhere before.

The next morning as Yesenia and her mother were washing clothes together, she said. "Mama, I dreamed last night that I was in heaven with Jesus and the angels. It was so beautiful up there. Jesus invited me to help the angels sing." She added wistfully, "I want to go to heaven."

Yesenia's mother looked startled, but she did not say anything. In their country, the Dominican Republic, dreams are very important to the people. *What can such a strange dream mean?* Mama wondered.

The days before Christmas were busy. Yesenia's mother took a small machete, cut branches off a low scrubby bush, and tied them to a broomstick. Yesenia used the broom to sweep the yard until the hardened dirt was clear of leaves, trash, and twigs. The furniture was carried onto the porch and all the inside walls of the house were scrubbed and hosed off. Mama pulled some clean curtains out of storage to replace the ones that had been hanging in the doorways of the bedrooms and along some of the walls.

There would be a feast on Christmas Eve. Yesenia's father built a wooden frame and gathered firewood to roast a fattened pig. The pig was kept in a wooden pen behind the house. Yesenia's mother would cook a big pot of rice and beans. She would make Russian salad and green salad, yucca topped with onions, and French bread. There would be dishes of apples, grapes, pears, raisins, and candy on the table.

Yesenia's older brothers and sisters would be home from the city for the evening. They would bring fireworks to add to the celebration. There would be music and festivity.

The day before Christmas, Yesenia's mother decided to go to town to buy a few more supplies. She and Yesenia started out on foot. After they had walked some distance, a motorcycle drove up beside them. It was a neighbor boy. "Do you want a ride?" he offered.

"Thank you," replied Mama. "Take Yesenia and drop her off at her aunt's place in town. I'll keep walking on foot." The motorcycle sped away, leaving Mama behind.

As Yesenia and the neighbor boy approached town, they neared a road grader that was smoothing out a side street that sloped sharply uphill. Suddenly the driver of the grader realized that his brakes were failing. The grader began to slide toward the main street. The driver saw the approaching cycle and desperately blew the horn and made motions, but the cycle driver did not seem to understand. He pushed the accelerator a little more and tried to speed up.

The grader rumbled down the hill into the main street. It hit the cycle with a sickening crunch. The driver flew off his cycle and landed in a heap ten feet away. But Yesenia was pinned under the huge wheel of the grader. The people who lived nearby heard the commotion and began to rush to the scene.

"Back up! Get off of her!" they screamed. Numbly the driver backed up and leaped off the grader to see if the girl was alive.

Yesenia lay terribly still. Someone felt for her pulse. There was none.

Someone else bent over her and listened for breathing. There was none.

The driver of the cycle was in better shape. His leg was broken, but he was conscious. "Let's take them to the hospital," someone said urgently. "Does anyone have a truck we could use?"

"Oh!" A sharp cry came suddenly from the back of the crowd. Yesenia's mother had slipped up unnoticed to peer curiously over the shoulders of the onlookers. "My baby! What happened to my baby?" she gasped. She pushed through the crowd and dropped to her knees beside her daughter. "Who will help me take her to the hospital?" she questioned desperately.

That night there was no Christmas Eve fiesta at Yesenia's house. Instead, a crowd of family members and friends came to mourn with the bereaved. They took most of the furniture out of the house. Yesenia was dressed in her white dress and placed in a wooden coffin. Candles burned beside the coffin and flowers lined the side of the room. In the next room, rows of chairs were set up for the family. Outside, backless benches and chairs were set up under a big blue tarp.

The neighbor ladies made hot coffee and a few men dared to set up a domino game off to the side. The sobs of Yesenia's mother and her older sisters and aunts were heard throughout the night. Occasionally, there was a commotion when someone was overcome with grief and fainted or became hysterical.

The Christians came and sang for a while. Then the pastor shared a short meditation and led in a prayer. The people listened respectfully because of the testimony that Yesenia had left.

In a far corner, a wise old man sat and watched everything.

He had known Yesenia and her family for years. "Her mother said that she dreamed about heaven before she died," he said to whoever was listening. "Maybe she knew that she would soon go there. She was headed in the correct direction. Yesenia was walking on the right road," he said. "She was walking on a better road than her family. Maybe if she had grown up, she would not have been able to stand alone. God knows what is best. He took her while she was innocent."

His companions nodded. "She lived like an angel here—and now the angels took her to heaven. Yes, God knows what is best."

Estefeni's Birthday Parties

True story

It was Estefeni's fifteenth birthday. A very special one! In the Spanish culture the fifteenth birthday calls for a celebration called a *quinceañera*. It can be almost as large as a wedding. The party includes lots of food and drink, a big cake, music, and dancing. The celebration announces to the girl's friends that she is now eligible to date.

But the party had barely started and already Estefeni's head ached. The music seemed to be rocking the house. Her friends were dancing and drinking. What was supposed to be the greatest birthday party was the worst birthday party of her life.

Oh Lord, Estefeni began praying within her heart, *I really do not want to be here. This music is terrible. How could it be that I once loved it? Look at the way my brother is acting with his girlfriend. It is shameful! What can I do? The more they drink, the more terrible the party will become. Tell me, Lord, what to do.*

Estefeni had recently become a Christian, and this party made her miserable. There was a church service tonight and she hated to miss it. *Why not just slip out the door?* she thought. *With all this music and commotion, I'll likely not be missed until the party is over—and the party is supposed to be for me!*

Estefeni stepped out into the night and strolled down the path to the road. She left her friends and family to celebrate her birthday the way they liked. She just didn't belong anymore. Things that once had seemed fun now seemed foolish. And not only that, she knew they were sinful and she wanted no part in them.

> Ointment and perfume rejoice the heart: so doth the sweetness of a man's friend by hearty counsel.
> Proverbs 27:9

She slipped quietly into the church and sat on a chair at the back. The service had started and she didn't want to draw any attention to her late arrival. After the service, she found her new Christian friends Denia and Flora.

"Oh, it's terrible. They're having my *quinceañera* party at home. They're drinking, and the music and dancing are wild. I just couldn't stand to stay any longer," Estefeni explained. "I slipped out of the house, and it's hard telling when they will miss me."

"They're celebrating your birthday without you!" Denia stifled a giggle.

"Whatever will your parents say when they find out you are

missing?" Flora asked.

"I think Mama will understand when I explain. I just felt so out of place that I had to leave," Estefeni said.

"It's good you left," both girls replied at once.

"You don't feel you belong because now you have the Spirit of God living in you. Their music, dancing, and drinking are from the spirit of Satan," Denia said.

"Then you don't think I did wrong by leaving?" Estefeni asked worriedly.

"Oh, no!" Flora exclaimed. "You did what a Christian should do. We are so glad you came to church. Come with us to practice singing with the youth."

"I think I will. My head feels much better. Thank you for understanding and for helping me," replied Estefeni. "I will need to leave for home by 10:30. Then the party will be over, and I don't want my parents to come looking for me or worrying about me."

Estefeni joined in the singing with all her heart. She felt a quietness and peace inside. This was where she should be and what she should be doing. Estefeni left for home with a much lighter heart. *I surely hope Mama will not think me ungrateful for leaving the party. But somehow, I think she will understand.*

As soon as Estefeni left, Denia and Flora shared with the others why Estefeni had arrived late and why she appeared upset. "I think *we* should have a birthday party for her," Denia suggested.

"Yes, yes," everyone agreed.

"We want her to know what a Christian birthday party is

like," added Flora.

So, a week later the Christian youth and their parents gathered for a different kind of birthday party. Denia had sewed six new dresses so that all the girls, including Estefeni, would be dressed alike. The boys bought a big cake, and several of the mothers had prepared food.

Estefeni arrived at the party with her parents. The group enjoyed the good food, cake, and punch. No blaring music or loud arguing shattered the happiness. The laughter and talk was pleasant and peaceful. The youth sang and shared testimonies. They encouraged Estefeni and each other to live for God.

Toward the end of the party Estefeni's parents stood up. They had something to say. Her mother began, "We were not very

Sometimes Mirrors Lie

happy with Estefeni when she disappeared from the *quinceañera* party we planned. Neither have we been happy about many of the changes she has made. But after seeing your happy faces and hearing your joyful voices, I want to thank you for being Estefeni's friends. I think I am beginning to understand—and I can now be thankful for the changes she has made."

Estefeni's father continued, "Yes, we are glad she is a part of this group. All of the birthday parties we held for our children have been rowdy and uncontrolled. But you all have had a nice time this evening in such a peaceful way. I have never seen anything like this. It is the best birthday party I have ever seen."

For Estefeni, it was one of the best days of her life! How wonderful it was to have friends—true friends who cared about her relationship with God. Friends whose behavior pointed her parents to God's path of righteousness. Friends who loved her enough to give her a *real* birthday party.

A Clash of Cultures

Part One: Africa—Two Houses or One?

Schoolteacher Tobias is more cultured and well-to-do than many of his fellow Africans. He struggles to mesh his culture with God's commands, but he chooses to follow God wholeheartedly. Tobias is a pillar and blessing to the church. This is a true story.

"I think it is time we migrate," Tobias said to his wife. Millicent knew what her husband was talking about. In the African culture "migrating" meant leaving your father's *dala*, or circle of huts, and starting your own.

"That is a wonderful idea," she replied, a smile lighting her eyes. To begin their own *dala* would mean more independence and the freedom to do things the way they preferred.

But Tobias had a problem. He had been married before and his first wife had died. According to the local religious beliefs, he would have to build a house for his first wife before he built a house for Millicent.

"I—I don't know what to do," he stammered to Millicent. He really did not want to put the subject before her, but Millicent guessed what her husband was thinking.

"I know what to do," she replied. "Let's build our house and forget about the house for your first wife. She is dead and gone. We are members of the church of Jesus—we are no longer slaves to our culture." In Millicent's mind there was no problem.

In Tobias' mind, however, a storm raged. How could he please God and also please his people? How could he be a part of God's kingdom and still remain a part of his culture? It just wasn't as simple as Millicent made it sound.

On the day of the house-raising, he succumbed to the clan and to culture and to superstition. He would build two houses and they would use them both. That way his unsaved relatives could be satisfied that his first wife had a home (though there was no way that the dead woman needed it) and his family could have a home away from his father's *dala*.

As the building day progressed, Pastor Eric and the church brothers saw what was happening. "We cannot help with this project," Pastor Eric said. Then he and the church brothers simply left the building site. Tobias also disappeared, leaving his wife in tears.

That night Tobias did not sleep well. Millicent spent much

of the night in prayer for her husband.

The next morning, Sunday morning, Tobias told his wife, "I am a sinner! I am not going to church. I am going to leave the church."

Immediately Millicent fell on her knees, praying for her husband. Soon several of his children came and begged him to go along to church. And of course, the church people were praying and pleading for Tobias to come through victorious, although he didn't know it at the time.

Through wisdom is an house builded; and by understanding it is established:

Proverbs 24:3

The Spirit of God worked, however, and Tobias finally decided to go to church after all.

He sat close to the front. He barely waited for testimony time until he was on his feet. As Tobias spoke, Silas, a brother in the church, interpreted.

"I lied to myself by saying that one house was going to be for cooking and the other one for the children to sleep in. I knew one was really a house for my first wife. I told my wife that I'm a sinner. I told her, 'I'm not going to church. I'm just going to leave the church.' My wife went down on her knees and started praying for me." He was nearly in tears as he spoke.

"My son came and tried to encourage me," Tobias continued, sobbing. By this time Silas was crying too hard to interpret, his face in his hands.[1] "My little son and daughter, about three and five years old, were even trying to get me to go to church. My whole family was trying to get me to go. I am sorry for my behavior and lack of faith in God. I am sorry for lying to myself. I am sorry for fearing the shunning of my clan. I am sorry for denying Jesus."

Everyone in the church rejoiced that Tobias had chosen the path of obedience. They knew there would be other cultural and superstition issues to face, but facing this one head-on had made Tobias stronger for the next time.

○ ○ ○ ○ ○ ○ ○ ○ ○ ○ ○ ○ ○

Part Two: America—Style or Simplicity?

Perhaps we Americans do not understand the strong pull of culture and superstition. It is intense—one of the strongest, most dreadful things the people in Africa must fight. But what about American peer pressure? What about being in style versus living a life of simplicity in America?

Brent came home from school very dissatisfied. "Mom, why can't I have a pair of Levi's and a matching jacket? Dustin came to school with another new pair and they look so neat. And Levi's is a good brand that lasts for a long time. I'm tired of cheap Walmart pants! I'm saving my money. When I have enough, may I buy what I want?" Brent looked pleadingly at his mom.

Mom's eyes filled with sadness and displeasure, and Brent

hung his head. Why didn't she understand?

"You know, Brent," Mom began, "we have discussed this problem of wanting what others have. The Bible says, 'And having food and raiment let us be therewith content.' You have food and clothes and many more things that millions of people do not have. Jealousy and envy are sin, and discontentment is a terrible sin of ingratitude.

> Hear thou, my son, and be wise, and guide thine heart in the way.
> Proverbs 23:19

"But Brent," Mom continued, "what troubles me more is your desire to look sharp, to be in style, and how you seem to overlook the principles of modesty and good stewardship."

Silence hung between them as Brent pondered Mom's words.

"So the pants are tight and you call that immodest?" he finally asked. He didn't really need a verbal answer. "I suppose Levi's pants and jackets are rather stylish," he added after a bit. "I'll try to remember what you told me, Mom. I do want to dress modestly."

Mom's eyes showed her joy. "It takes a lot of God's wisdom, son, to live in this world and not get caught in the snares of peer pressure. But with God's help it is possible," she encouraged.

Guard that Tongue

Based on a true incident

Carrie and I were straightening some storage room shelves for Miss Butterick and tossing outdated materials from the social studies classes. We had already turned in our work for the day and Miss Butterick wanted to keep us busy, I guess.

Carrie pulled down a box and began sorting through it. "Look, here are some old test papers. I didn't know teachers kept these from year to year." She shuffled through them. "Wow, Debbie got a D on this one!"

"Let me see," I said. Then I laughed. "She wrote that apples are one of the main things you see when you visit Washington, D. C. Must be she got it mixed up with the state of Washington." I read a little more. "And listen to this; she says Santa Anna is the capital of New Mexico. Does that girl need help or what?"

Carrie didn't answer so I looked up to see what had her attention. I could have sunk through the floor when I saw Debbie standing in the doorway. Her face was red and she looked as though she were about to cry.

"Oh, uh—hi, Debbie," I said, wondering if she'd heard my unkind words.

"Miss Butterick says it's time to put things away. Class ends in five minutes," Debbie said. She quickly turned and left.

Carrie and I exchanged guilty looks. "Do you think she heard me?" I asked.

"Probably," Carrie said. "She came in while you were reading her answer about New Mexico."

> There is that speaketh like the piercings of a sword: but the tongue of the wise is health.
> Proverbs 12:18

Oh, no, I had done it again. It seemed like I was always saying something without thinking. Now I had hurt Debbie's feelings. It would be a wonder if she'd ever talk to me again.

I really didn't enjoy hurting people. I just didn't think. My mouth went into action before my brain turned on, I guess. As a Christian I really believed in the golden rule, and I knew I had done something to Debbie that I wouldn't want her to do to me.

This wasn't the first time I had spoken out of turn and hurt someone. I remembered passing on some gossip about Emma, who had just moved to our area. On her first day of school, someone told me her dad was in prison for stealing money from his employer. On the way home, I mentioned this to another friend and she told more folks. Pretty soon everyone was talking about it. As it turned out, Emma's father had a name similar to the name of a man who had made news because of his stealing—but it wasn't Emma's father at all.

One of the girls asked Emma outright, "Is your dad in prison?" Emma had been completely bewildered. Of course she said no, but she was hurt that people believed the rumor. I felt guilty because I'd been part of the group spreading false information. And even if Emma's dad had been in prison, I knew it wasn't right for me to gossip about it.

Now, after the incident with Debbie, I knew I had to shape up. That evening I finally did what Mother had been encouraging me to do for a long time. I got out my Bible and, using the *Strong's Concordance,* I found the words she had given me to look up.

In the book of Proverbs alone, the word "mouth" appears 50 times. I went through my Bible and marked all the "mouth" words in red. Then, using a blue pencil, I marked all the "tongue" words. There were 19 of them. Next I took my green pencil and marked the word "lips"—42 of them! Indeed, Proverbs talked a lot about the use of the mouth. It even named the different kinds of tongues—and only three of the names were good: wise, wholesome, and soft. Most of them were bad: lying, froward, foolish, naughty, perverse, backbiting, and flattering. A number of verses spoke of the kind of tongue or lips that God hates.

I was feeling rather foolish and depressed. I had a big problem with my tongue and I needed help. So right then and there I breathed a prayer to God to help me watch what I say.

I asked Him to help me control my tongue. I truly didn't want to make others feel badly. And I surely didn't want to have a tongue that displeased God or lips that He hated.

But how was I going to mend things? Should I just be extra nice to Debbie and pretend nothing had happened? Or should I be straightforward with her and apologize? If I did, what could I say? "Sorry, Debbie, I called you a dummy but I didn't mean it."

Well, I hadn't actually called her a dummy. I think I said she needed help. Maybe that was it. Maybe Debbie really *could* use some help. Maybe I could invite her over to my house and we could drill on things like state capitals and historic dates and that sort of thing.

The following day at lunchtime, I looked for Debbie. She had just finished eating her lunch. She took her cafeteria tray back and was heading for the door when I stopped her. "Debbie, I'm going outside. Want to go with me?'

I wouldn't have blamed her if she'd said, "No," but she came along with me and we went out to sit on the front steps. I plunged in right away. "Debbie, I'm sorry. I have a big mouth and often say things I don't mean. I want to apologize. Will you forgive me?"

Debbie didn't answer for a minute and I held my breath. What if she just got up and walked away? I deserved it.

"It's okay," she said. "I know I'm not a very good student. I try, but things just don't stick in my mind. The counselor told my folks I should have private tutoring—but we don't have the money." She bit her lip. "I'm afraid I'm not passing in two classes this year, social studies and English."

I took her hand and smiled. "Would you let me tutor you? I've done it before. Last year I tutored a boy in English, and the summer before that I helped a girl who had a failing grade in math. They both passed with Bs. I want to be a teacher, anyway, so it's good training for me. We'd both benefit. How about it? It's free."

For the first time, Debbie smiled, then she said, "I'd like that. When can we start? Today?"

Carrie and I had a shopping trip scheduled, but I quickly changed plans. "We sure can. Want to come over to my house after school? We can get in an hour or two and see how it goes. After that, we could do it twice a week or whatever works."

> The tongue of the wise useth knowledge aright.
> Proverbs 15:2

When we went back into the school building, I felt much better. Yesterday I hadn't acted much like a Christian—but I sure hoped that today I had become more Christ-like. And from now on, I want to think twice, speak once, and pray often.

—Marie Latta

Quit or Grit?

"I wish I could make some money before Mom's birthday on Friday," Charlene said as she and her friend Danette walked down the snowy sidewalk. "I'd like to buy her a new pair of gloves. Her old ones have a hole in the thumb."

"Maybe we could do some errands here in our neighborhood," Danette suggested. "I could use some extra money too. Let's go house to house and ask if there are any jobs we can do. I just hope we don't get a snow-shoveling job, though that looks like the most obvious possibility. I'd rather help someone bake cookies in a nice warm kitchen," Danette said with a laugh.

"I like your idea," Charlene said. "Let's start right now." They were near the Masons' house, so they turned in at the nicely shoveled walk.

"Hello, girls. How are you today?" Mrs. Mason asked as she opened the door.

"Fine, thank you," Charlene said. "We wondered if you had any errands or small jobs we could do. We'd like to make some money. I want to buy some gloves for my mom for her birthday."

"Let me see." Mrs. Mason paused. "I did have some work this morning, but my son Jim did it for me."

"All right, Mrs. Mason. Thanks anyway," Charlene said.

He that speaketh truth sheweth forth righteousness: but a false witness deceit. Proverbs 12:17

"That's something we didn't think of," she said as they went on down the street. "Most families have children to do their errands."

"Then we'll find somebody who doesn't have children, maybe Mrs. Fowler," Danette said. "She lives alone and her grand-children live in Denver."

The girls crossed the street to Mrs. Fowler's house and saw Mrs. Fowler shoveling snow from her walk.

"What brings you girls out this wintry day?" she asked.

"We're looking for jobs to make some money," Charlene said.

"That's nice," Mrs. Fowler said. "I'm tired and was wishing someone would take over this shoveling. I just started the walk and still need to do the driveway and sidewalk out in front. I'd like it done today. How much would you girls charge?"

Charlene and Danette looked at each other. They hadn't thought about that. "We don't know how much to charge,"

Sometimes Mirrors Lie

Charlene said.

Mrs. Fowler paused. "Last time I had it done, Bob Holmes charged twenty dollars. Does that sound all right to you girls?"

"Ten dollars each! That's wonderful," Charlene said. "Is that okay with you, Danette?"

Danette nodded.

"Fine," Mrs. Fowler said, laying down her snow shovel. "There's another shovel in the garage."

The girls began shoveling. Soon Danette stopped and leaned on her shovel. "I'm getting tired," she said, "and it's more work than I thought. We haven't got much done and we still have a lot to do."

Charlene looked around. Danette was right. It was slow work but the walk was halfway cleared of snow and they had also shoveled the porch and steps.

A few minutes later Danette put down her shovel. "I guess I'm not very good at this kind of thing. I don't want to do it anymore. Let's quit. It isn't fun."

Charlene stared at her friend in amazement. "We agreed to do the job for Mrs. Fowler. We can't quit before it's finished."

"Why not?"

"Because we said we'd do it." Charlene continued to shovel as Danette watched. She searched for words to encourage her friend. "Danette, do you remember what we learned in church about keeping our word?" Charlene asked. "Proverbs 6:2 says, 'Thou art snared with the words of thy mouth, thou art taken with the words of thy mouth.' When we say we will do something, we need to do it or our words will catch us and make us a liar."

"Oh, come on, Charlene!" Danette protested. "Don't be so serious about such a little thing. If you want to slave away, I guess you can."

"When I feel like quitting, Mother always says, 'It's easy to

Sometimes Mirrors Lie

quit, but keeping on requires grit,'" Charlene said as she tossed a big shovelful of snow off the walk.

"Well, I'm quitting. I guess I don't have the grit! Let Mrs. Fowler find someone else to do it." Danette leaned her shovel against a tree. "Anyway, I just remembered I told Julie I'd come see her new kitten this morning. See you later." Danette waved and walked off down the sidewalk.

Charlene watched in disbelief as her friend walked away. She found shoveling even less desirable when she had to work alone, but she had started a job that must be finished. She would have liked to see the new kitten too, but she kept shoveling. An hour later she had finished the walk, the driveway, and the front sidewalk. She felt tired and ready to flop down in the snow and rest.

"Ready for some hot chocolate?" Mrs. Fowler called from her porch.

"Yes, thank you," Charlene called back. "Just let me take these shovels back to the garage."

Sitting in Mrs. Fowler's pleasant kitchen, Charlene relaxed and sipped her hot chocolate. She bit into one of the oatmeal cookies Mrs. Fowler set out. "These are so good," she said.

"Why, thank you. It's my mother's recipe. Maybe someday after school, you can stop in and I'll show you how to make them," Mrs. Fowler said. "But right now, we need to settle our bill." She took money from her purse and counted out eighteen dollars for Charlene. She laid two dollars aside. "I'll call Danette and have her stop by for her pay."

"Oh, but we were going to split the money," Charlene said.

"Ten for me and ten for Danette."

"Yes, but you were going to split the work too. Since Danette didn't do her fair share of the work, she doesn't deserve half the pay. The Bible says 'the laborer is worthy of his hire.'[1] I'm paying what I think your work is worth. I'm sure Danette will understand when I explain it to her."

> Thou art snared with the words of thy mouth, thou art taken with the words of thy mouth.
>
> Proverbs 6:2

On Friday morning Charlene couldn't wait any longer. She brought her gift to her mother.

"You are so thoughtful," Mother exclaimed, pulling one glove onto her hand. "I can wear these to church with my new coat. But where did you get the money to buy them?"

So Charlene explained.

When Charlene finished, Mother smiled. "I love the gloves," she said, "and I'm so pleased with you. When you agree to do a job, you keep your word. I think the Lord is pleased too.

"Remember, if you commit to doing a job and then walk off without finishing, you are actually being deceitful. Keeping your word may cause you tiredness or even pain, but it always leaves you with a good conscience."

"It's easy to quit, but keeping on requires grit," Charlene quoted.

"That's right!" Mother agreed with a smile.

—Marie Latta

---

[1] Luke 10:7

33

A Dog for Doug

At first Doug thought the tapping was his friend Joe. Strange, though, that Joe would come at suppertime. When he opened the door, he saw a little beagle looking up at him with big sad eyes and wagging its tail.

Doug let the dog inside. "Come on in, pal," he said and then called out to his dad, "Just see what God has sent me!"

Doug scratched the dog's ears. He'd always wished for a dog, even prayed for one. And didn't it say in the Bible, "Ask and you shall receive"? Dad had told him, however, that it was better to pray that God would take care of his needs and not ask for something specific. Besides, Mom didn't like dogs. She'd been bitten when she was a little girl.

Dad came to the door, and Doug looked up into his face.

"Dad, I've always wanted a dog—and now he's come! I think I'll name him George. He wants to stay, Dad, see?"

"Wait a minute, son," Dad said. "For one thing, you'd better make that Georgia. This little hound is a female and she's going to have puppies soon. For another, she belongs to someone else. She isn't yours."

Doug looked at Georgia, who sniffed about the living room, investigating, and then curled up near the fireplace. What would Mom say when she saw her?

He didn't have long to wait. Just then Mom entered the room. "Supper's ready. Get washed, Doug, and . . ." Her voice trailed off as she noticed Georgia. "Where did that dog come from?"

"She pawed at the door and I let her in. Can't she stay a little while?" Doug pleaded. "See how nice she is . . . and it's going to rain."

Sure enough, raindrops were already trickling down the window pane.

"Well, just until the rain stops," Mom said.

Doug hurried through supper and went back to the dog. "Hi, Georgia," he murmured, lying down beside her in front of the fire. Georgia wagged her tail.

Dad came into the living room and sat down to read the evening paper. "She seems well-trained," he noted. "Doesn't tear around or climb on the furniture."

Later Mom joined them. "Is it still raining?" she asked as she peered out the window. Then, in answer to Doug's unspoken question, "You can fix a box for her in the garage, but leave the back door open. Maybe she'll decide to return to her home."

Sometimes Mirrors Lie

Doug stood up. "Maybe her owners don't want her any-more," he said, though he didn't believe that. A beautiful dog like this would be missed.

The next morning, Doug hurried to the garage to see if Georgia was still there. She didn't come to meet him, but he heard her tail thumping against the box. With her, nestled close, were five squirming puppies.

"Mom! Dad! Come see Georgia!" he called excitedly.

Mom and Dad came out to the garage. "Oh, my!" Mom exclaimed. "Now what are we going to do?"

"First, we'd better offer Georgia some breakfast," Dad said.

"We don't have any dog food," Doug said.

"Let's give her some bread and milk," Mom suggested.

Georgia ate greedily. Doug petted her and glanced at the puppies. He wanted to hold one, but he decided it would be better to give Georgia some time alone with her new family. Anyway, he had to get ready for school.

Time passed slowly for Doug at school. On the way home, Joe and Craig stopped by to see Georgia and the puppies. Doug led his friends to the garage and Georgia rose to greet them. "I'll get her some fresh water," Doug said. "Don't pick up the puppies. Just look."

Neither of the boys had any idea where Georgia had come from. No new families had moved into the neighborhood and no one at school had mentioned a lost dog. Doug was glad. If no one claimed her, maybe he could keep her.

Her manners were perfect. She didn't jump on the sofa or beg at the table or shed hair on the carpet or do any of the things

Mom didn't like but expected a dog to do.

After supper, Doug went out to see Georgia and the puppies. He patted a puppy and Georgia didn't seem to mind so he picked it up. Its eyes were tightly closed and it made whimpering sounds. Doug wished he could stay there all night, but

Sometimes Mirrors Lie

he heard his mother calling.

"Okay, Mom," he said, setting the puppy down.

Dad was standing by the telephone, holding the newspaper open. "Looks like we've found Georgia's owners, Doug. Read this." He handed the paper to Doug.

Lost Wed. near Oak and Elm, female beagle with black collar. Answers to *Penny*. Call 555-1650. Reward.

Doug blinked back tears. "Lots of beagles have black collars, probably."

Dad was already calling the number. "Hello, this is Roger Taylor at 15 Carlton Drive. I'm calling about your ad. We found a dog. Can you describe yours?" He paused, listening. "Yes, five pups Wednesday night. Sounds like your dog. When would you like to come for her? Tomorrow evening is fine. Certainly. Good-bye."

Sadly, Doug turned to go back to the garage but his father stopped him. "I know you're disappointed, son—but think how you'd feel if she were yours. Mr. Johnson said she chased a motorcycle and must have gotten lost. They live about a mile from here. Their little boy, Tommy, has been worried. Tommy's in bed already or they'd come for her now."

Doug nodded. Dad was right. He'd been right about the way to pray too. But for a while it had seemed as though Georgia was an answer to his prayer. "I'll take some food out to her now," he said.

Georgia wagged her tail when she saw Doug. "Guess I should call you Penny," he said. He set the dish down and scratched behind her ears while she ate.

The next day after school Doug went to the garage as soon as he got home. He wanted to spend every possible minute with Penny. He let her into the house and she followed him to his room and lay on his rug while he changed clothes. "I can't see what bother you'd be," he said. "Even Mom says you behave."

All too soon it was evening and a blue car was turning into the drive. A man and woman and little boy got out. Doug opened the garage door and Penny dashed out to welcome her family. The little boy gathered her up in his arms. "I missed you, Penny," he said.

Dad led the way into the garage. A few minutes later they loaded the puppies, box and all, into the back of the car and Penny jumped in too.

"Thanks, young man, for taking good care of Penny and her litter," Mr. Johnson said, reaching for his wallet. "You have a reward coming."

Doug shook his head. "No thanks, I don't want a reward. I liked taking care of Penny. I wish she were mine. I've never had a dog."

Be thou diligent to know the state of thy flocks, and look well to thy herds.
Proverbs 27:23

"Would you like one?" Mr. Johnson asked. "In six weeks these pups will be weaned, and I'll give you the pick of the litter."

Doug was silent. Sure, he'd like one, but what would Mom say?

He blinked when he heard Mom speaking. "Thank you, Mr.

Johnson. If Doug will train his dog to behave as well as Penny, we'd like a pup. He's proved he can take care of a pet."

"Come over in a couple of weeks," Mr. Johnson said as he got into his car. "The pups will have their eyes open then and Doug can choose the one he wants."

Doug finally found his voice. "Thank you," he said. "Bye, Penny." He tried to swallow the lump in his throat.

Dad put his hand on Doug's shoulder. "How about that? Your own dog at last."

"It's great, Dad," Doug said. "And isn't it kind of like an answer to prayer, even though I stopped asking for it?"

"Yes, son, I think it is," Dad said.

—Marie Latta

Juanita's Prayer

As told by a missionary

Juanita opened the house door and stepped out into a bright Sunday morning. Dew glistened on the grass and the brilliant orange flowers that had fallen from the flame tree in the corner of the yard. A few fluffy clouds were scattered in the vast blue sky. A flock of noisy parrots chattered in the mango trees behind the house.

Juanita and her family lived in Belize. Their small wooden house was built on posts high above the ground and covered with a tin roof. Last year before Christmas, her mother had painted the house dark blue. The railing around the porch kept her baby brother from falling the eight feet to the ground.

Juanita stepped down the wooden stairway and between the posts into the space under the house. The posts supported a hammock and an array of wash lines. Beside the wringer washing machine, she found an empty white bucket. She filled the bucket at the water faucet in the front yard and carried it to a small wooden structure behind the house that served as a place to bathe.

Juanita wanted to wash up before she went to church today with her mother and baby brother. After she bathed and dressed, she filled another bucket and poured the water into a washtub. She climbed the steps into the house again to find her little brother, Giovanni.

Ma was in the kitchen at the back of the house. She came to the kitchen doorway with flour on her hands. Giovanni was toddling behind her, holding on to her skirts. "Ma, I'll give Giovanni a bath," offered Juanita.

"That would be helpful," said Ma with a smile. "As soon as you're done, come up and eat something."

Soon Juanita was sitting at the table with her freshly bathed little brother. She watched her mother swiftly pat out flour tortillas and bake them on the comal.[1] The delicious smell of hot tortillas made her mouth water.

Her mother buttered two tortillas and put them on a plate in front of her. "When did Pa come home?" Juanita asked her as she bit into one of the tortillas.

"He came home at midnight. I'll leave breakfast here on the table for him because he won't wake up until after we are at church." Her mother put the last tortilla on the comal as she

---

[1] A comal is an earthen or metal griddle used in Latin American countries.

Sometimes Mirrors Lie

added with a sigh, "He promised me last week that he would stop drinking, but his friends talked him into it again."

Within the last year, Juanita's father had been drinking more heavily. His drinking caused a financial strain on the family. Even money meant for food and clothes was spent on rum. There was never any extra money at Juanita's house.

Juanita slipped her feet into her worn rubber sandals and picked up her Bible. Her mother lifted Giovanni and they left the house together.

Juanita loved Sunday mornings. She loved to go to Sunday school and hear the Bible stories her teacher Miss Rosa told. Juanita did her best to learn the Bible memory verses. Miss Rosa also taught the children lovely songs.

As they reached the white block church building, Pastor David met them at the door. "Good morning, Miss Ana," he greeted Ma warmly. "Welcome, Juanita. God bless both of you."

Ma sat near the back of the church, but Juanita went to the front. She sat beside Karima, whose shiny black hair was braided into many thin braids. Each braid had a brightly colored ribbon tied to it. Karima wore a new white dress and black dress shoes with white lacy socks. When Juanita saw the shoes, she pushed her own feet back under the bench. She did not want the other girls to notice her worn out sandals.

Wine is a mocker, strong drink is raging: and whosoever is deceived thereby is not wise.
Proverbs 20:1

I wish I would have some shoes, she thought.

Soon the front bench was full of girls. Juanita looked down at the feet of all of her friends and felt sadder. Every girl on the bench had a nice pair of sandals or dress shoes. Every girl—except Juanita.

I am not like the other girls, she thought. *I am the only one who doesn't have nice shoes to wear to church.*

Juanita still felt sad during Sunday school, but she listened attentively as Miss Rosa told a story about two poor boys who lived with their mother. Their father had died, owing money to a creditor. The creditor wanted to take the boys as his slaves because the mother could not pay the debt. Then God performed a miracle through His prophet Elisha.

The prophet told the mother to borrow jugs and jars from her neighbors. She gathered many jugs and jars and set them on the floor of her house. She filled one jar, then another, and still another, from a jar of oil that she had. God multiplied the oil until there was enough to fill all the borrowed jugs and jars. Then the mother sold the oil and made enough money to pay the debt. Now she could keep her boys with her. How happy she must have been!

"God took care of those two boys and He cares about each of you," finished Miss Rosa. "God knows what you need, children. He wants us to trust in Him and take our needs to Him."

The cool of the morning had been replaced by the heat of the tropical noon sun as Juanita and her mother trudged home from church. Their feet stirred up little puffs of dust.

"Ma," Juanita said, "can you buy me some new shoes? These sandals are so ugly and worn out. I don't like to wear them to church anymore."

Her mother looked sad. "I know you need some new shoes," she said. "I wish I could buy some for you. But Juanita, we don't have any money for shoes. I'm sorry, but when your pa spends money on drink, there is never enough for . . ." Her voice trailed off.

Later that afternoon Juanita remembered the story of the widow and her two sons. She decided to pray secretly for some new shoes. She knelt beside her bed and prayed to her heavenly Father for some new black dress shoes. Then she stood up with a happy feeling inside. Somehow God would answer her prayer.

Several weeks went by. One day Ma called, "Juanita, could you please go out to the main road and wait for the tortilla lady to go by? I need some corn *masa*[2] to make *empanadas*[3] for supper." Ma gave Juanita two round dollar coins.

Juanita took a little umbrella to shield her from the sun's rays and obediently walked two blocks to the main highway. Twice a day, the little green jeep would go by, beeping the horn. The horn was calling anyone who wanted to buy fresh hot corn tortillas or ground corn *masa*.

Juanita came to the highway in front of Miss Alexa's house. Miss Alexa was an older woman from the church who lived alone except for a grandson whom she was raising. Her husband had left her years ago and her children lived in the States.

Miss Alexa was sitting on her porch and fanning herself with

---

[2] Masa is a dough made from ground corn.

[3] Empanadas are pastries that are filled and folded in half.

a newspaper. She smiled and waved to Juanita. "Come and drink some juice," she invited. "My grandson picked a bucket of berries from my tree and I just made some juice. We'll watch for the tortilla lady together."

Juanita and Miss Alexa were sipping juice and chatting when Miss Alexa remembered something. "My daughter came from the States last week. She left some black shoes that are too small for her children and said I should give them away. Do you want to see them? They might fit you."

Juanita's eyes lit up. "I've been praying for shoes," she answered shyly. "I would like to see them."

Miss Alexa laughed happily. "I'm sure they'll fit you if God sent them for you!"

Juanita slipped her feet into the beautiful black shoes. Sure enough, they fit perfectly. "Thank you, Miss Alexa," she said with a wide smile. "You helped God answer my prayer."

On the way home, Juanita carefully carried the corn *masa* and the shoes. "Thank you, dear God, for answering my prayer," she whispered. "Thank you for these nice shoes."

She walked faster. She could hardly wait to show her mother what God had given her.

My Sister Michelle

True story

Katie looked up from the garden where she and Michelle were pulling weeds. Someone was riding a bike up the street. As the bike came closer, Katie realized it was her new friend Brenda.

"Let's quit for now, Michelle," Katie said. "Go into the house and get yourself some lemonade."

Michelle smiled. "All done?"

"Yes, now shoo." Katie swatted playfully at her sister.

Michelle disappeared into the house only seconds before Brenda turned into the drive.

"Hi," Brenda said. "You busy?"

"I was," Katie answered, "but I need a break. Have a seat on the porch and I'll get us some lemonade, okay?"

"Sounds good." Brenda plopped onto the glider on the porch.

Katie grinned. Brenda had just moved here. Katie had met her at church last week and liked the way Brenda had answered the Sunday school teacher's questions and took part in discussion. They had discovered they lived two blocks apart. Katie had said, "Come over sometime," and now here she was.

Katie went into the kitchen. She hadn't mentioned Michelle to Brenda. Michelle always needed explaining to new acquaintances. She could say, "This is my sister Michelle. She is always smiling. She's eighteen but has the mind of a six-year-old." That would cover it, but she'd like to find a better way to tell Brenda.

"How're you doing, sis?" she asked Michelle as she poured two glasses of lemonade and arranged cookies on a plate.

"Okay," Michelle said. "May I have a cookie?"

"Sure, take two." Katie shoved the cookie jar across the table. "But stay in here and eat, okay?"

Michelle nodded as Katie went out, carrying a tray.

Brenda rose when she returned. "Can I give you a hand?"

"No, thanks." Katie set the tray down and sank into a chair next to Brenda. "Well, how do you like our little town?"

Brenda sipped her lemonade. "Fine, so far. I was hoping you'd give me a tour. Do you have anything going on for the next hour or two?"

"I'd love to, Brenda. But Mom's shopping and I have to stay with my sister."

"I didn't know you had a little sister," Brenda said.

It was the perfect opportunity. "She's not exactly little," Katie began.

"I know what you mean," Brenda said. "My brother's nine

Sometimes Mirrors Lie

and I have to watch him sometimes. He can take care of himself but my folks don't want him left alone." She finished her cookie. "Well, maybe you'll show me around some other time."

Katie felt miserable. She wasn't ashamed of Michelle, at least she didn't think so, but she couldn't think of a good way to tell Brenda just yet.

"Thanks for the goodies." Brenda stood up. "I'd better be going."

Katie walked with her to her bike. As she was getting on, Michelle came running out. "Katie, telephone."

Katie glanced from Michelle to Brenda. "Excuse me, I'll be right back." She ran into the house. The call was from the dentist's office, confirming an appointment. When she returned, Brenda and Michelle were chatting like old friends.

"Brenda, this is my sister Michelle," Katie said. "I see you've met."

"Yes," Brenda said. "Michelle was telling me about going to the zoo. We both like polar bears."

"And monkeys," Michelle added. "Aren't they funny, Brenda?"

"They sure are," Brenda agreed. "The last time we went to the zoo, one stuck his hand over the drinking fountain and squirted me."

Michelle's delighted laugh rippled across the yard.

"I'll be shoving off," Brenda said, "but I still want that tour."

"Tour? What tour?" Katie wondered. "Oh, you mean showing you the town. How about four this afternoon?"

Brenda started down the drive. "Fine. See you then. Bye, Katie. Bye, Michelle."

It had been so easy. Brenda hadn't needed any explanation. She had seen that Michelle had special needs and it hadn't fazed her. *Why can't I see it that simply?*

That afternoon Katie sat waiting on the porch when Brenda appeared. She rose and started down the walk. "Before we get sidetracked, Brenda, I want to tell you about Michelle," she began. "It wasn't fair to just spring her on you like that."

"Why? We got along fine."

"Well, most people feel uneasy around handicapped folks."

"Now wait," Brenda said, "just because Michelle has a problem doesn't make her all that different. Maybe she can't do some things others can, but I admire her for managing so well." She paused. "I guess I should tell you—my mother is handicapped."

Katie's thoughts whirled. What must Brenda think of her?

"Mom had a stroke last year," Brenda continued. "She uses a wheelchair and her speech is hard to understand, but she is getting better every day. I'd like you to meet her."

"I'd like that," Katie said. They walked on half a block before she found the words she knew must be said. "I'm not ashamed of Michelle, Brenda."

Brenda nodded. "I understand. You want to protect her from criticism. I was like that with Mom at first. I was so protective I wanted to keep her in her room all day. Then Dad gave me a good talking-to. He said Mom needed to get out and see people."

"Does she want to?"

"Yes, she loves going grocery shopping where they have motorized carts so she can pick out the food. We take her every week. And she enjoys visitors. She was always busy with church and school activities before the stroke, and she needs to get back in the swing of things."

They stopped in the park and sat on a bench. "Brenda, I'm so mixed up," Katie said. "When I was younger, I didn't realize Michelle was different. Now I compare her with other girls her age, and I question why God lets things like this happen. Why didn't He give Michelle a healthy brain like other people? What will happen when she gets old? She'll always need someone to take care of her. Will it be me?" She paused and looked at Brenda. "I'm sorry. I'm talking too much."

> A merry heart maketh a cheerful countenance: but by sorrow of the heart the spirit is broken. Proverbs 15:13

Brenda took her hand. "It's all right. I wish I had answers, but I don't. I'll tell you what Dad told me, though." She grinned. "One of Dad's little sermonettes, as he calls them. Want to hear it?"

Katie wiped away a tear. "Sure."

"Okay." Brenda took a deep breath. "Mom used to put together jigsaw puzzles, those giant thousand-piece ones. She'd keep at it, adding a piece of blue sky here, green bush there, and eventually, this beautiful picture would emerge. Dad says we're all like little puzzle pieces and sometimes we can't see why God made us the way we are, but He has a plan and we all fit into our own special place, like pieces of a puzzle."

Katie smiled. "I feel better, just hearing you say that." She paused. "I'm going to pray that God will show me how to help Michelle instead of being angry because she's not like everyone else." She stood up and Brenda rose too, and they began walking again. "I don't have any idea of where to start, but I'm going to try."

"I have an idea," Brenda said. "Where we lived before, our church teens had a project. Our Sunday school teacher also taught special ed and she told us that people with special needs ought to have more recreation. So we gave a monthly party and invited the disabled young people in our town. In summer, we played softball or volleyball in the park, served refreshments, and had a devotional period. During the winter, we played indoor games like checkers and ping-pong. Everyone enjoyed it and some of our guests began coming to regular church services."

"Our Sunday school class could do that!" Katie said.

"Let's look into it," Brenda said. "But right now, let's go on downtown. I want to visit the courthouse and look at that octagonal building. I'm interested in architecture."

"Great," Katie said, walking with a spring in her step. "And afterward, maybe we can stop by your house and I can meet your mother."

—Marie Latta

Cockfights and Surrender

As told by a missionary

Rosa's bare feet stirred up tiny clouds of dust as she hurried up the trail toward her grandmother's small house. Her heart felt sad. If only Papa and Mama would stop fighting. If only Papa would stop wasting money on drink and gambling at the cockfights! If only Mama would cook some good meals. If only there were more food in the house!

Rosa let out a deep sigh. "If onlys" accomplished nothing. She had once heard the missionary say that people should bring their "if onlys" to God and He would take care of them. Right now Rosa truly wished she knew how to give her "if onlys" to God.

"Hola, nieta,"[1] Rosa jumped at the sound of her grandma's

---

[1] *Hola, nieta* means "Hello, granddaughter."

voice coming from the garden.

"*Hola, Abuela,*"[2] replied Rosa. "Oh, *Abuela,* I'm so hungry. May I come to your house for some rice and beans? Papa used all his pesos to buy rum again."

Grandma Anita sighed. "Yes, you may eat at my house. Where is Enrique?"

"He's gone fishing. He thought you could sell some fish in the village and give him the money to buy some food," Rosa replied.

"Yes, I know a store that will buy the fish. Maybe that is a good plan so you children can have something decent to eat. I don't understand how your father can keep on drinking as sick as he feels from the AIDS," Grandma said with another big sigh.

"Do you think you could get the church people to come to our house for a church service next week?" Rosa asked. "It seems to help calm Mama. She is talking of leaving Papa again."

"Yes, I think we can arrange to have a service at your house. The missionaries are always willing to help where they can," Grandma answered.

Rosa shivered as she remembered the time her mama had left home, thinking that maybe Luis, her man, would be shocked and stop drinking. But instead he began drinking more and more. Poor Enrique and Rosa had to fend for themselves while Mama was gone. Every week Rosa had needed to take their school uniforms to the community pila[3] and scrub them herself.

---

[2] *Abuela* is the Spanish word for grandma.

[3] A pila is a communal water fountain often found in Latin American towns.

Sometimes Mirrors Lie

Grandma Anita had tried to help all she could, but the drunken Luis had often told her to go home and mind her own business.

After several months, Mama Julia had realized that home wasn't the worst place in the world to be, so she had decided to come back. She did miss her children, and Luis was a kind man when he was not drunk.

Rosa did not want her mama to leave again. She would pray harder, as the missionary said!

o o o o o o o o o o o o o o o

Rosa was twelve now and she knew she should not cry like a baby, but still the tears ran down over her brown, smooth cheeks. Should she go to Grandma with her problem? Always there seemed to be problems. Either they did not have enough food, or Papa and Mama were fighting, or Papa was losing money at the cockfights, or the witch doctor was insisting on his crazy charms and rituals when someone was sick at the house. The witch doctor brought things like red string to tie around the wrist, supposedly to fight sickness. Rosa would always tear the red string from her wrist as soon as he was out of sight. She knew it would not keep sickness away. At the mission, she had learned that only God can keep sickness away and only He can heal. Oh, why was there always something

His own iniquities shall take the wicked himself, and he shall be holden with the cords of his sins. Proverbs 5:22

wrong at their house?

Only God can heal! Her thoughts rang in her ears. Why did she sit here crying? Why hadn't she thought to take her problem to God? Surely He could do something about it. Nevertheless, she needed her grandma's help. The missionary had said just this past Sunday, "Where two or three are gathered together, God is there." She and Grandma would make two and they could pray together.

Rosa's bare feet ran down the dirt path to Grandma's house. She rushed in the door without even calling out. Grandma sat in her rocking chair, knitting.

"Well, it looks like you have some important news, flying through the door like that!" Grandma said with a smile. Then she noticed the tear-streaked face and sober look. "Tell me, child, what is wrong?"

"Oh, *Abuela!* Mama had a baby girl, but Mama is very sick. The witch doctor wants to go to the government hospital and do his crazy treatments and I don't want him to touch Mama," Rosa exclaimed in one breath.

"Let's pray, Rosa," Grandma said, kneeling by the chair.

"That's what I came for," Rosa replied, falling down beside her.

The two poured out their hearts to God. They prayed for the sick mother, the beautiful new baby, and even the witch doctor. As they got up from their knees, Rosa exclaimed, "Oh, I feel so much better. I know Mama will die sometime because of AIDS, but I hope she will first give her life to Jesus. And I hope she will live until the baby grows up."

"Yes, my child," Grandma answered. "Come now, let's walk to

the missionary's house and ask them to pray for your mama too."

At last Mama came home from the hospital, bringing with her a dear black-haired baby with big brown eyes. How Rosa loved baby Angelica! For a week, she stayed home from the fields to help care for Mama and Angelica. Rosa was glad to

be out of the hot summer sun. She was thankful that God had heard their prayers. The witch doctor had stayed away from the hospital and God had brought Mama and the baby home safely.

However, Mama was still sick and weak. In fact, Rosa needed to stay home and help all summer. Baby Angelica grew sweeter every day—or so the family thought! How thrilling to see her first bright smile of recognition, then to hear her laugh and say "goo, goo." Even Papa and Enrique loved to hold her and play with her.

Since Rosa could not get away to attend the mission services, the pastor and some of the village Christians came to their little house and held services. After every service, the pastor pleaded with Mama Julia and Papa Luis to surrender their lives to God. Finally, after one service, Julia and Luis fell to their knees and asked God for forgiveness. A new light shone from their eyes as they got up from prayer. Rosa was crying because she was so happy. Everyone was crying for joy, except Angelica, who was smiling from Rosa's lap.

How different life became in the little house with the dirt yard and bright hibiscus flowers beside the door. Papa came home early from work and even brought money in his pocket. Mama tried her best to have a nice meal prepared, though she was growing weaker every day.

One evening after supper Papa said, "Julia, I think we should get married now that we are Christians." Julia looked at him with a bright smile. "You have been my 'woman' for a long while, but now I want to make you my 'wife.' "

Enrique spoke up, "But why, Papa? Most of our people just take

Sometimes Mirrors Lie

a woman and live with her and she becomes his wife that way."

"Our custom is not God's way," Papa replied.

Mama happily agreed with Papa and they asked the pastor to come to their house to perform the ceremony. Mama was too weak to walk to the church. A friend from the church brought her a nice dress and a veiling.

"Oh, Mama, you look so nice," Rosa exclaimed after Mama had tried on her new clothes to see how they fit.

Luis and Julia were married the following Sunday at their home. How happy everyone was. The women brought food and there was a wonderful meal. After everyone left, Mama was exhausted and went to rest in bed, but never had she gone to bed happier.

Julia seldom got out of bed after that wonderful day. She grew weaker and weaker, and finally she died. She left behind a sad family—and yet they were a much happier family than they had ever been before.

The family struggled for a few weeks, and then Papa decided that Grandma Anita should take Baby Angelica. How Rosa cried when her baby sister left, but she knew that she and Enrique were needed to help their papa in the fields. She would be brave and help him all she could. He was such a different man now that he loved God.

In three short months Papa had to go to the hospital. One day the children went to visit him. "Dear children," he said weakly, "I will die soon, but I will go to be with your mama! How good God is that He forgave us before we died. Please live for God so you can meet your mama and me in heaven."

About a week later Papa Luis died. Now there were three orphaned children. There was much sadness and crying at the funeral. Yet there was quiet joy and wonder at the grace of God in saving this couple before He took them home.

Another change came into the lives of the children. It was decided that a neighbor would take care of baby Angelica, and Rosa and Enrique would go to live with their grandma.

Grandma Anita took the children to church and they attended a Christian school. They were sad and life was difficult at times, but they knew their parents were happy and waiting for them in heaven. God had a plan for Rosa's life, and she would follow His plan.

Ice for Mrs. Leh

True story from China

Mrs. Leh tossed restlessly on an old pallet on the dirt floor in a dark corner of the little hut she called home. She was burning with fever, and the August day was hot. Not a breeze stirred the mulberry trees along the canal or relieved the smelly air of the sickroom. The flies buzzed noisily. It was far past noon, but the Chinese landscape still simmered in the heat.

The missionary doctor on his daily rounds of mercy appeared in the open doorway of the dingy hut. The patient's face brightened, and she stretched her thin, yellow hands toward him as he knelt beside her and breathed a word of earnest prayer to the Great Healer.

While the doctor ministered to her physical needs, he noticed that her eyes were fixed on his face with eagerness.

Then she opened her lips and spoke. "Tell me, doctor, does God want His children to have what is good for them?"

The doctor beamed. "Oh yes, Mrs. Leh. He is a loving Father, and will not withhold any good thing from those who ask in faith."

Mrs. Leh's face grew more eager and her hot fingers clutched his hand. "Doctor, wouldn't ice be good for me?"

"Yes, my good woman, ice would be very good for you, but you know it is hundreds of miles to the nearest ice factory. We must try to not want the impossible."

The doctor's answer did not satisfy this simple Chinese woman. She had a great need and a simple faith. What did she care for nature's laws? "But is not God all-powerful?" she insisted.

The doctor shifted uneasily as he felt himself being driven to what he considered dangerous ground; but there was only one reply to make, and he made it with a steady voice and with a trembling heart. "Yes, nothing is too great for Him."

The woman's fingers tightened and her glassy eyes searched his face for final satisfaction. "Then, doctor, will you go home, gather the missionaries, and have them beseech God to send me ice to cool my fever?"

The missionary man of science felt himself being hurled with tremendous force against the promises of God. Only last week this simple woman had been a heathen, but now she had become a woman of great faith.

Did he believe in prayer? Of course he did, otherwise he would not be a missionary. But to ask the great Creator of the universe to send ice on a blazing August day to please a fevered patient seemed presumptuous. And yet, as God's representative, he could not desert the woman in her time of trouble. He would do anything to help her.

Then the truth broke upon him. How much more would his Heavenly Father hear the prayer of His trusting child, she who was turning from heathen darkness? Yes, he would go home, humble his intellectual pride, and pray for the impossible.

The doctor's wife, noting his downcast face as he entered the mission compound, ran to meet him. He told her of the desperate challenge to his faith and the disastrous results that might follow should the prayer not be answered.

The Lord . . .
heareth the prayer
of the righteous.
Proverbs 15:29

To his surprise, his wife responded joyfully, "How lovely! I have just been longing for a real adventure in faith and here it is! Of course we are not going to be disappointed. I will send out the prayer call at once."

These missionaries had stood together many times in spiritual emergencies. As the messenger ran from door to door, they dropped their ordinary work and hurried to the doctor's house. There they took counsel together. They reviewed God's promises. They prayed as only they who have gone to the ends of the earth at His command can pray. They pleaded that His name might be glorified among the heathen, and that the faith of this suffering woman might be honored. A great burden of intercession fell upon them and they forgot time and place until they were suddenly aroused by terrific claps of thunder—as though the heavens would split.

As they rose from their knees, a heavy rain was pouring and a wild wind was blowing. Suddenly the intensity of the storm increased, and it sounded as though millions of pebbles were being dashed against the windows. When the doctor cautiously opened the door, great hailstones rolled across the floor. Outside they were banked in glittering heaps of coolness on the sills and about the steps.

"The ice! The ice! I knew it would come." The doctor's wife clasped her hands together in solemn happiness.

The doctor hurried into the hall for his hat and umbrella. Then he put his head back through the doorway long enough to say, "Please return thanks." He ran through the flooded streets, making his way along the wet cobblestones to the home of his patient.

The storm had almost spent itself, leaving a delightful freshness in the air. The wind was still struggling through the bamboo branches. The mulberry trees had been riddled by the hail, and bits of green leaves were mingled with the ice lying in small drifts on the ground.

As the doctor entered the doorway to the humble hut, the setting sun broke through a cloud and threw a ray of light across the face of Mrs. Leh. Her expression was changed to radiant peacefulness, as though the Master had been there Himself with His healing touch.

Her hands were full of melting hail, placed there by her awed and wondering friends who were standing in groups

Sometimes Mirrors Lie

talking about the "Jesus doctrine." At the sight of the doctor, she broke forth joyously, "See, doctor, God has sent me ice from heaven. Now I shall be well. Tell my friends about the 'Jesus doctrine,' for now they will also believe!"

"I hate being different"

True story

Kurt fished in his pocket for his lemon drops. That familiar feeling was creeping up on him again. He'd planned to just shoot a few baskets, but when Jim came by, the few had lengthened to a half-hour workout. As he popped the candy into his mouth, Jim asked, "Aren't you going to share?"

"Oh, sure, sorry." Kurt held out the package for Jim. Sometimes he forgot the simple courtesies. Now would be a perfect time to tell Jim about his diabetes and low blood sugar, but the words just wouldn't come. *Hey, Jim, in case I start acting dippy, would you be a friend and tell me to eat candy or take a glucose tablet? See, I have this problem that causes my blood sugar to take a nosedive whenever I get too much exercise, don't eat enough lunch, or just get tense. Then I need something sweet right away.*

No, that wouldn't do. And if he couldn't discuss it with Jim, who he'd known since fourth grade, he sure didn't want to talk about it with other people.

Kurt had been just fine all his life, up until last August. Then suddenly he was thirsty all the time. He was so tired he fell asleep doing his homework, and when he stepped onto the scales he saw he'd lost seven pounds. His mother had been worried and scheduled a doctor's appointment for him.

From that day on, his life had changed. When he came out of his week-long stay in the hospital, he was no longer Kurt, a whiz at tennis, the fellow everyone applauded for his computer expertise, the one everyone sought for help with math. From that day on, he was Kurt the Diabetic.

Give instruction to a wise man, and he will be yet wiser: teach a just man, and he will increase in learning.
Proverbs 9:9

It wasn't the diet—giving up desserts and counting starches and stuff—that he disliked so much. It wasn't even the shots of insulin four times a day. What he really hated was being different. He couldn't stay late at the gym after school anymore—he had to eat his meals at proper times. He couldn't make a meal of potato chips and a malt—not a good idea for anybody, but it had been fun once in a while. He also felt strange about having to do blood tests before he took his insulin. Not that it was anything to be ashamed of, but he was the only one in his class who did it, so he usually went off by himself to prick his finger. No, the worst thing about diabetes was that it set him apart.

Sometimes Mirrors Lie

That night at dinner, his father asked, "How are things going at school, son?"

Kurt's answer was automatic. "Great."

His mother glanced at him. "You don't sound great."

"Really, I'm okay," Kurt said.

But the next day at lunchtime, Kurt wasn't okay. He'd already tested his blood sugar and taken insulin. He was heading for the cafeteria when he felt a bit dizzy, something that often occurred when his blood sugar was dropping. He felt in his pocket for candy and then realized he hadn't replaced the package after giving Jim the last pieces yesterday. *I need something to eat,* Kurt thought, *and I need it now.*

Jim was ahead of him on the stairs. "Hey, Jim, do you have any candy" he asked.

Jim shook his head. "No."

Kurt felt himself beginning to sweat. "I need to eat something. I've had my insulin and I'm starting to feel as if I'm going to pass out. What am I going to do?"

Understanding filled Jim's eyes and he held up a sack. "I've got my lunch. Would a peanut butter sandwich help?"

Gratefully, Kurt took the food Jim held out. "Thanks, I'll eat your lunch if you'll let me buy yours in the cafeteria."

Sitting at the lunch table later, Jim said, "Why didn't you tell me about being diabetic? It's no big deal."

Kurt smoothed back a lock of hair that flopped forward. "I just hate being the only one who's different."

Jim grinned. "You're different, all right. You've got the biggest feet in school." Without waiting for Kurt's response, he continued. "If you think about it, we're all different. My dad says God didn't want everyone to be the same. Too boring. So He made some of us short, some tall, some fat, some thin. Some folks have asthma, or break out in hives when they eat strawberries. Being diabetic isn't fun, I'm sure, and I'm not trying to minimize it, but you're still the same old Kurt."

"Big feet and all?" Kurt smiled. "You're right, Jim. Thanks for reminding me."

Jim pushed back his chair. "We'd better get going or we'll be late for English class."

"Speaking of English, do you have your oral report ready?"

Jim shook his head. "I haven't decided on a topic. How about you?"

Kurt sighed. "Nothing."

"Why don't you talk about diabetes? You could educate us all and maybe get an A."

"I'll think about it," Kurt said.

The more Kurt thought about Jim's idea, the better it seemed. By Monday, he was ready. He took along his blood testing kit, a syringe, and bottle of insulin. He explained to the class that his pancreas was not producing insulin, so he had to inject insulin and follow a special diet. He also told them if he acted strange—well, stranger than usual, he said with a grin—he needed to eat something immediately. Preferably something sweet or starchy, like glucose tablets, orange juice, bread, milk, or candy.

After class, Stephanie came up to Kurt in the hall. "That was the most interesting report we've had yet," she said. "My mom's diabetic too, and we follow her diet. Lots of fresh fruit and veggies. Actually, I think we eat better than most of my friends."

"Your mom's diabetic? I never would have known. My cousin takes piano lessons from her. He says she's terrific."

"Yes, the way Mom puts it, she didn't ask for diabetes, but she's got it, so she might as well accept it. But she didn't do anything to deserve her musical talent either, and she's glad God gave her that."

Stephanie suddenly turned to Kurt. "I think each of us is a special combination of God-given talents—and problems, too—all wrapped up in one package. Take me, for instance. I'm left-handed, with red hair and green eyes. I'm good in English, not so good in math. I am an adopted child and I detest Brussels sprouts. Each of us is one-of-a-kind, but we're all God's children."

"I like Brussels sprouts," Kurt replied, smiling, "but I get what you're saying."

As they walked down the hall, Kurt thought, *Okay, so I'm different. But I like the way Stephanie says it better—I'm one-of-a-kind. That's not so bad.*

—Marie Latta

A Bunny and a False Witness

True story

"Father, Father, my bunny is gone!" Thomas exclaimed, wiping his eyes to keep tears from running down his cheeks. "My pretty spotted Nutmeg is gone!"

Father put down the paper he was reading and pulled nine-year-old Thomas up on his knee. "Tell me—" Father began, but was interrupted by the banging screen door and a loud, unhappy voice.

"He left the cage door open," twelve-year-old Allen accused.

"I did not!" Thomas declared.

Allen continued talking. "Cinnamon got out too, but I found him. I'm going to put my bunny in a separate cage, so I won't have to worry about my little brother letting him out again."

"I don't think that will be necessary," Father said, "especially if

Nutmeg is lost. You boys go look carefully in the barn, and be sure to check at the blackberry bushes back by the pond. Bunnies like blackberries and the nice hiding places the vines make. You'll probably find Nutmeg somewhere." Father patted Thomas on the head and wiped the muddy tears from his cheeks. "Perhaps you'll be more careful from now on."

"I was careful! I didn't leave the door open!" Thomas said stoutly.

"You did," Allen declared.

"I didn't!"

"Boys, arguing will not help find Nutmeg," Father said firmly.

"It's no use looking for Nutmeg," Thomas moaned as soon as they were out of the house.

"Oh, come on. I found Cinnamon. Maybe we can find Nutmeg too. Don't give up yet." Allen felt sorry for Thomas even if it was his fault the bunny was gone.

In the barn the boys looked behind the hay, on top of the hay, under the tractor, in buckets, everywhere. But Nutmeg wasn't to be found.

Thomas crawled up on a hay bale where he could think.

"Come down from there," Allen commanded. "Let's go look in the berry vines before it gets dark."

"No, I don't want to go back there. Nutmeg never knew anything about those blackberry vines, and I'm sure he didn't go back there," Thomas said stubbornly. "I know where Nutmeg is. He's at Jeff's!"

"At Jeff's? Where's that? You're just a fraidy-cat and don't want to go back to the pond," Allen challenged.

"I am not afraid! And you know who Jeff is—Jeff Brown, the

neighbor boy. He stole Nutmeg, that's what he did. I'm sure of it."

"How can you say Jeff took Nutmeg? Prove it to me," Allen demanded.

"Well, first, Jeff liked Nutmeg very much. He said he wished he had a bunny like him. He even said that maybe someday his father would have enough money to buy him a bunny."

"All that doesn't prove a thing!" exclaimed Allen.

"Just let me finish," Thomas said impatiently. "See this." He pulled a small blue car from his pocket. It was covered with tiny pink dots.

"That's Jeff's car," Allen said. "No one else around has a funny little car like that. Where did you get it? Did you steal it?"

"Allen Eberly, you know I don't steal! I found this car about five feet from the rabbit cage. This is my evidence."

"When did you find it? And why didn't you tell me about it before?" Allen questioned his brother like a judge questioning a prisoner.

"I found it in the barn right after we discovered Nutmeg was gone. I didn't tell you about it because I didn't feel like it," Thomas said with a toss of his head. "This car proves Jeff stole Nutmeg."

A false witness shall not be unpunished, and he that speaketh lies shall not escape.
Proverbs 19:5

"It does no such thing," Allen declared, still unwilling to believe their friend would steal anything. "Jeff could have dropped it when he was here on Wednesday."

"But that was two days ago," Thomas replied. "One of us

certainly would have seen the car if it had been lying there for two days."

"Well, maybe you're right," Allen said slowly. "Maybe Jeff did take Nutmeg. But I sure wouldn't tell anyone else, just in case he didn't."

"I guess I *will* tell. Isn't it our job to warn the others at school so they'll be on the lookout? We don't want everything we own to be stolen."

"Allen! Thomas! Come for supper," Mother's voice called from the house.

Thomas stuffed the car into his pocket and jumped from the hay. Allen was already racing toward the house.

As soon as the boys were inside, Father asked, "Did you find Nutmeg?"

"No," the boys answered together. And without being told, they hurried to the bathroom to wash. Both were hoping Father wouldn't ask where they had looked.

During the table blessing Father prayed that God would help the boys find Nutmeg, if it was His will the bunny be found. Thomas squirmed. Allen cleared his throat.

As soon as Father finished praying, Thomas pulled the blue car with pink dots from his pocket. Allen kicked him under the table, but it was too late. Father saw the car and seemed to notice some problem between his sons.

"Where did that come from?" he asked.

"It was—was near—the rabbit cage," Thomas began. He was afraid his story wouldn't convince Father, but he told it as confidently as possible.

"So, you see, I'm sure Jeff took Nutmeg. This car proves it!" he finished forcefully.

Thomas and Allen looked at each other and then started passing food. Nothing looked or smelled good. Why should a missing bunny ruin a fellow's appetite?

When supper was finished, Father reached for his Bible. He leafed through it thoughtfully. Usually Father read a chapter from Romans, the book they were now reading during family devotions. But tonight Father read verses from one place and then another.

"Do violence to no man, neither accuse any falsely."

"Thou shalt not raise a false report."

"Whoso privily slandereth his neighbor, him will I cut off."

"Thou shalt not bear false witness against thy neighbor."

"A false witness shall not be unpunished, and he that speaketh lies shall perish."

The room was very quiet for some time and then Mother spoke to Father. "You know, accusing someone falsely is the same as stealing his reputation."

"That's right," Father replied. "And that's the worst thing we can steal from anyone. Of course, all stealing is wrong, but a person's reputation is easy to destroy and very hard to rebuild."

Thomas sat with his head down. Sure, he knew they were talking to him. But they were wrong this time! Jeff had stolen Nutmeg.

Saturday and Sunday passed without mention of Jeff or Nutmeg. At school on Monday, Thomas and Allen avoided Jeff as much as possible. They made sure all the other boys knew

Nutmeg was mysteriously missing. And then Monday evening, who should come riding in the lane but Jeff Brown!

Thomas and Allen could hardly believe their eyes. "Well, the nerve of that boy!" Thomas exclaimed under his breath.

"Hi, fellows," Jeff greeted the boys as his tires skidded to a stop on the gravel drive and he jumped from his bike. "You didn't happen to find my little blue car with pink dots around here, did you?"

"Sure did!" Thomas replied, trying to hide his feelings. "Found it in the barn near my bunny's cage." Thomas handed the car to Jeff; then suddenly he had an idea. "Say, you didn't happen to get yourself a bunny yet, did you?"

"Why, yes, I did. My uncle brought it to me Saturday for my birthday. It's brown spotted, almost like yours." Jeff hesitated, and then asked, "But how did you know?"

"Oh, I didn't. I was just guessing." Thomas looked at Allen, and Allen looked at Jeff.

"What's up anyway?" Jeff questioned, puzzled by their suspicious manner.

"Nothing," Thomas replied.

"Well, I have to hurry home. I need to help load chickens for market. See you tomorrow."

As soon as Thomas and Allen arrived at school the next morning, Thomas called a group of boys around them. "When Jeff comes ask him where he got his bunny," he said with a knowing look. "Ask him what color it is too."

The boys looked at each other. "You don't mean Jeff is a thief," one boy said.

"I didn't say so," Thomas spoke up quickly. "Ask Jeff himself."

When Jeff left school that evening, he left alone and with his head hanging.

"Serves him right," Thomas told Allen, trying to ease his conscience. "Who wants to be friends with a thief?"

"But what if he didn't steal Nutmeg?" Allen said uncertainly.

"What do you mean?" Thomas replied. "We know he did it."

As soon as the boys arrived home, Father put them to work, and Nutmeg and Jeff were forgotten once more.

"I want you to carry the garbage out to the driveway and then mow the rest of the lawn, Thomas," Father instructed. "And you, Allen, should clean out the chicken coop. Then, before it gets dark, I want you both to go back to the pond and look for duck eggs around the blackberry vines. Mother thinks the ducks must be laying someplace back there."

Thomas finished mowing lawn in record time. He hurried out to the chicken coop. "Come on, slowpoke. I'm ready to go back to the pond."

"Well, I'm not," Allen answered. "Either you'll have to help me or you'll have to go back to the pond alone."

"Oh, I'll help you, if you hurry," Thomas said grudgingly.

"I knew you wouldn't go back to the pond alone," Allen laughed. "What are you afraid of?"

"I'm not afraid of anything. I just don't like it back there with those tangled berry vines all over the place."

The boys worked in silence. At last they finished and hurried toward the pond and the berry vines. Allen went in one direction and Thomas in another, looking for duck eggs.

Suddenly Allen shouted, "Thomas, come quick! Come and see what I found."

Thomas walked slowly toward his brother. He couldn't imagine anything exciting in these old berry vines.

"Look!" Allen exclaimed, pointing toward a brown object tangled in the vines.

> A man that beareth false witness against his neighbour is a maul, and a sword, and a sharp arrow.
> Proverbs 25:18

Thomas's mouth fell open. "Nutmeg!" he exclaimed. He knelt on the ground beside the limp form of his bunny. Blackberry vines were all tangled around the nutmeg-colored fur. It was plain to see the bunny had been dead for several days.

Thomas looked up at Allen and said slowly, "If we would have come back here on Friday when Nutmeg was first missing, we might have found him alive. And if we had found Nutmeg, I wouldn't have blamed Jeff. And if I hadn't blamed Jeff . . ."

"You might as well forget all the *ifs,*" Allen interrupted his brother. "What's done is done."

"I guess you're right." The brothers headed for the house, but Thomas was thinking hard.

He swallowed to clear the lump from his throat. "I—I—have to tell the boys at school that I was wrong. And—I—need to ask Jeff to forgive me. I'll sure be glad when it's over." He paused. "And I'm going to do my best to make sure this won't happen again."

Amy and the Nail

A true experience from the 1930s, when doctors still made house calls and antibiotics were rarely used.

Amy was excited! Her family was planning a trip to Lancaster. A trip was special for the Zooks. With eight children in the family, they seldom all went away at the same time. Tomorrow was the day!

Amy skipped up the back stairway to her room. Mother had told her to pick out a dress for the trip. This was a new and important task for her. Always before, Mother had picked out the clothes she wanted Amy to wear. As Amy took her pink dress with yellow flowers from the closet, Mother called up the stairs, "As soon as your room is straightened, I want you to come down and help me pick some strawberries for supper.

"Pick strawberries!" Amy exclaimed to herself. "I hate picking strawberries!"

Mother called again from the bottom of the steps. "Be sure you don't come down the front stairway, Amy. There are nails sticking up from where the carpenters were tearing out boards that need to be replaced."

Amy tried to clean her room, but her hands didn't work well because her mind was busy thinking how she could get out of picking berries.

After a long time Mother called again. "Amy, it's time to come down—right now!"

Amy headed for the front stairway. She'd slip out the front door and hide in the barn. She was halfway down the steps, walking carefully around the protruding nails, when Mother suddenly appeared at the bottom of the steps.

"I told you not to come this way," Mother said. "You will need to be punished for your disobedience."

Frustrated and angry, Amy stomped her bare foot, once, then again. The second time down she cried out, "My foot! A nail! Oh!" She stood screaming, fastened to the step.

Quickly and carefully, Mother went up the steps and gently pulled Amy's foot from the nail. A stream of blood squirted from the wound. Several of Amy's sisters had gathered around by now and Anna quickly handed Mother a clean rag to wrap around Amy's foot.

Two of Amy's older sisters went to pick strawberries while Mother soaked and bandaged Amy's foot.

Amy was sitting on the couch with her foot up when Father came in for supper. "Well, well, what happened to my girl?" he asked.

Amy didn't look up into Father's face. With hanging head she said quietly, "I-I stepped on a nail on the stairs."

"But Amy, you knew the carpenters were repairing the front steps. Why were you there?" Father questioned.

After a long silence, Amy confessed through tears, "I was trying to sneak out of the house so I wouldn't have to pick strawberries. I-I got angry when Mother caught me, and I put my foot on a nail."

"*Put* your foot on a nail? Are you sure you weren't *stomping* your foot?" asked Father. "I've warned you about that bad habit, Amy. This time your anger really hurt you, didn't it? Anger always hurts on the inside—and sometimes on the outside." Father looked sadly down at her.

"Come along for supper," he said.

"I can't walk!" Amy cried. "It hurts too badly."

Father reached down, picked up his big girl and carried her to the table.

Just before bedtime, Mother looked at Amy's foot again. Angry red lines reached out from the wound. "Oh, this does not look good," Mother told Father. They agreed that they should call the family doctor. Though it was not office hours, the kind doctor said he'd be right out.

After the doctor arrived and examined Amy's foot, he looked from Mother to Father. "Could I speak with you privately?"

In the kitchen the doctor explained, "I don't want to frighten the child, but blood poisoning will start soon if you don't treat it immediately. You will need to sterilize a needle and dig into the hole every few hours to drain out the infection. She must stay off her foot for at least a week."

The doctor came back into the room with Mother and Father. He showed them what needed to be done. Through howls and tears, Amy began to understand the seriousness of her stubbornness. After the doctor left, Father carefully explained to Amy the necessity of draining the infection.

He also answered the unspoken question that had been worrying her. "You will not be able to go on the trip tomorrow, Amy. You must stay off your foot and it must be treated every three hours. Anna said she will stay home with you and take care of your foot. It is important that Mother goes with me. I am sorry that things have turned out this way."

Amy burst into tears. It was just as she'd feared. She would miss the wonderful trip she had been so excited about—and all because of one foolish act of disobedience!

That night Amy cried herself to sleep. The next morning she was a picture of gloom, and that didn't improve when Anna pierced and drained her sore foot before breakfast. The family had left before Amy was up.

All day Amy thought of the fun the family was having. Then she thought of poor Anna who had to stay home because of her. "It's not fair!" Amy exclaimed after Anna had cleaned her wound for the third time that day.

"What's not fair?" Anna asked sadly.

"It's not fair that you miss the fun of the trip just because of me. You so badly wanted to look for dress material for Karen's wedding. It plain isn't fair that you couldn't go!"

"Life isn't fair," Anna replied. "When we do wrong it often

affects others, and the innocent have to suffer with the guilty. I really am sorry I missed the trip, but I don't want my little sister to lose her leg either. Staying home will be worth it if you have learned your lesson. And thanks for thinking of me."

"I've learned my lesson all right. I'll never stomp my foot again!" Amy declared.

Anna agreed. "You are getting too big for that childish habit. But I hope, Amy, that willing obedience is the biggest lesson you have learned through this experience."

My son, despise not the chastening of the Lord; neither be weary of his correction: For whom the Lord loveth he correcteth; even as a father the son in whom he delighteth. Happy is the man that findeth wisdom, and the man that getteth understanding. Proverbs 3:11-13

Berries and the Hedge of Thorns

True story

"Lester, come on! This is the fourth time I've called you." Rita stood in the doorway of the living room with her hands on her hips. "We must get those blueberries picked before Mom comes home from town."

Lester slowly closed the book he was reading and looked blankly at his sister.

"I said we must pick the blueberries!" Rita repeated more loudly than necessary.

"Oh, yes, yes. I remember what Mom said at breakfast," Lester replied.

"Well, you certainly aren't acting as if you heard anything," Rita answered. She turned in the doorway, went to the kitchen, and grabbed a bucket. Lester followed slowly.

Rita hated it when her brother moved like one of the fat slugs that thrived in the wet Oregon climate, acting as if he had not a care in the world. Picking blueberries with him this morning was not going to be fun.

Rita and Lester each started on a row of blueberries. The rows seemed long this morning and the bushes were loaded.

They picked in silence until Rita suggested, "Let's sing. That always helps the work go faster. Why can't you pick faster? You're getting way behind me."

"Who feels like singing when his sister hollers, yells, and screams at him?" Lester retorted.

"Oh come on, Lester. I didn't holler, yell, and scream. Maybe I did talk too loud. Sorry! But you exasperate me when you move like a fat slug."

Lester hated that fat slug bit and his sister knew it, but he decided to give her a reminder and threw several blueberries at her.

"And you know Mom said, 'No throwing blueberries because it is a waste.' "

"Soft, squishy blueberries are a waste before I throw them," Lester laughed and threw several more.

"Stop it, Lester! Just look at the stains on my dress—they will not make Mom happy at all."

Oh my. Why do blueberries have to stain? Lester wondered. He would be in trouble. Suddenly he laughed out loud.

"Now what's so funny?" Rita asked.

"Oh, I just thought of that saying, 'Eating forbidden fruit always gets you into a jam.' Well, throwing forbidden fruit also gets you in a jam."

Rita had to laugh in spite of herself. She said, "And not picking the fruit can get you into a jam too."

"Well, it sounds like I'm in a jam all the way around." Lester looked up at the sound of crunching gravel and, sure enough, Mom was driving in from town.

Rita was at the end of her row and carried her full bucket across the grass to the drive.

Lester looked at his bucket and panicked. It wasn't even half full. He couldn't let his sister put him to shame like this. He must have been eating all the time he was picking, and his row was nowhere near being finished.

Suddenly he spied an empty bucket. He picked it up, carefully filled it half full with sawdust from around the base of a berry bush, then poured his picked blueberries on top. Now he had a nice full bucket.

Lester hurried into the kitchen and set his bucket on the counter and rushed out to the van to help carry in the groceries. Then he disappeared to the barn.

Lester stayed in the barn until he was called for supper. After a delicious meal of taco salad, the blueberries were passed around for dessert.

Dad said, "Say, Lester, what's wrong with you and the blueberries? You didn't take any,"

"I ate mine out in the blueberry patch," he said without looking up.

As soon as they were excused from the table Lester grabbed his book and went up the stairs two at a time.

He tried to read but his mind wouldn't stay on the book. Why had he been so stupid to think sawdust would hide his lack of berries? Why had he thrown berries when he knew he wasn't supposed to? Why hadn't he worked faster at picking?

The questions continued to torment him. Why was he always doing something wrong? Why couldn't he do right like Rita? It must be a lot easier for girls to do right than it was for boys.

Lester was dreading the call to come downstairs for family worship. Suddenly there was a tap on his door and Rita announced, "Dad said to tell you we will have our devotions privately tonight in our own rooms. He said we should be sure to read Proverbs 15."

Well, that was certainly unusual. At least he wouldn't get preached at tonight. Lester took his Bible and sprawled across the bed. He slowly turned to Proverbs 15 and began to read. His eyes lingered on verses 19 and 20. *The way of the slothful man is as an hedge of thorns: but the way of the righteous is made plain. A wise son maketh a glad father: but a foolish man despiseth his mother.*

His laziness in the blueberry patch was certainly turning into a hedge of thorns, he realized. He had felt his conscience pricking him ever since. Suddenly he felt very sorry for the sawdust, the blueberry stains, and the few blueberries in his bucket. He knew his father would not be glad about what had happened in the berry field. But did his behavior actually mean that he despised his mother? He certainly had acted foolishly.

Silently Lester slipped to his knees and asked God to forgive his laziness and foolishness. Then he climbed into bed and fell fast asleep.

Lester was awake early, dressed quickly, and hurried downstairs. He was ready to go out the back door when Mother stopped him. The time of reckoning had come.

"Lester, right after chores and before breakfast you may go pick the last row of blueberries, then come into the house and scrub out the stains on Rita's dress. It is in the washtub," she said quietly. "Then you may have breakfast. And be sure to thank your sister for sorting the blueberries out of the sawdust in your bucket."

Lester hung his head. When he looked up, he saw compassion in Mom's eyes. "Oh, Mom, I am so sorry for all the trouble yesterday with the blueberries. I will do better today," he promised.

"I forgive you, son," Mom said. "I am praying for you."

Lester quickly finished in the barn then went to the blueberry patch with a clean bucket swinging from his arm. He thought about that hedge of thorns he had created yesterday by being such an unwilling worker. *I'm going to get rid of that hedge of thorns today,* he determined. He picked blueberries with a will and was amazed at how little time it took when he really wanted to pick them.

Lester carried the full bucket to the kitchen and set

The way of the slothful man is as an hedge of thorns: but the way of the righteous is made plain. A wise son maketh a glad father: but a foolish man despiseth his mother.
Proverbs 15:19, 20

it on the counter. His stomach was growling from hunger but he knew he had one more job to do. At the washtub he found Rita's stained dress. This was a job he had never done before and he wondered how to go about it. He saw a bottle of stain remover sitting nearby. He called to his mother, "Am I supposed to use this stain remover on the dress?"

Mother came to the doorway and instructed. "Get the spots wet, then spray them with that bottle and scrub lightly with that brush. Rinse and see if the stain is gone. If you still see the spots, do the same process again."

Lester carefully followed Mom's instructions. His hungry stomach was urging him to move faster. Soon the spots were gone and Lester went triumphantly to the table for a delicious, big breakfast. He grinned at his mom.

"Thanks, Mom, for your love, help, and patience—and most of all for this breakfast!"

About the Author

After living in a house full of children and activity, Faythelma lives alone since her husband of forty-seven years passed away in 2008. They raised a family of nine and cared for over thirty children and adults in the beautiful hills of Estacada, Oregon.

Faythelma has been writing for over forty years. She did freelancing for twelve years, selling poetry, stories, and articles to religious magazines and Sunday school papers. She has also written junior Sunday school quarterlies for Christian Light Publications.

Books written by Faythelma are *Speedy Spanish Levels 1–3, Christian Ethics for Youth, School Days Devotional Praise, I Will Pass Over You, Sharpen UP, Reflections of God's Grace in Grief, Light Through the Dark Valley,* and *God's Grace in the Valley.* She compiled four Creative Touch bulletin board books for teachers and reprinted *Inspiration for Education*.

Faythelma welcomes responses from her readers and invites you to email her at becbooks4u@gmail.com. You may also write to her in care of Christian Aid Ministries, P.O. Box 360, Berlin, Ohio, 44610.

About Christian Aid Ministries

Christian Aid Ministries was founded in 1981 as a nonprofit, tax-exempt 501(c)(3) organization. Its primary purpose is to provide a trustworthy and efficient channel for Amish, Mennonite, and other conservative Anabaptist groups and individuals to minister to physical and spiritual needs around the world. This is in response to the command to ". . . do good unto all men, especially unto them who are of the household of faith" (Galatians 6:10).

Each year, CAM supporters provide 15–20 million pounds of food, clothing, medicines, seeds, Bibles, Bible story books, and other Christian literature for needy people. Most of the aid goes to orphans and Christian families. Supporters' funds also help to clean up and rebuild for natural disaster victims, put up Gospel billboards in the U.S., support several church-planting efforts, operate two medical clinics, and provide resources for needy families to make their own living. CAM's main purposes for providing aid are to help and encourage God's people and bring the Gospel to a lost and dying world.

CAM has staff, warehouses, and distribution networks in Romania, Moldova, Ukraine, Haiti, Nicaragua, Liberia, Israel, and Kenya. Aside from management, supervisory personnel, and bookkeeping operations, volunteers do most of the work at CAM locations. Each year, volunteers at our warehouses, field bases, Disaster Response Services projects, and other locations donate over 200,000 hours of work.

CAM's ultimate purpose is to glorify God and help enlarge His kingdom. ". . . whatsoever ye do, do all to the glory of God" (1 Corinthians 10:31).

The Way to God
and Peace

We live in a world contaminated by sin. Sin is anything that goes against God's holy standards. When we do not follow the guidelines that God our Creator gave us, we are guilty of sin. Sin separates us from God, the source of life.

Since the time when the first man and woman, Adam and Eve, sinned in the Garden of Eden, sin has been universal. The Bible says that we all have "sinned and come short of the glory of God" (Romans 3:23). It also says that the natural consequence for that sin is eternal death, or punishment in an eternal hell: "Then when lust hath conceived, it bringeth forth sin: and sin, when it is finished, bringeth forth death" (James 1:15).

But we do not have to suffer eternal death in hell. God provided a sacrifice for our sins through the gift of His only Son,

Jesus Christ. "For God so loved the world that he gave his only begotten Son, that whosoever believeth in him should not perish, but have everlasting life" (John 3:16).

A sacrifice is something given to benefit someone else. It costs the giver greatly. Jesus was God's sacrifice. Jesus' death takes away the penalty of sin for all those who accept this sacrifice and truly repent of their sins. To repent of sins means to be truly sorry for and turn away from the things we have done that have violated God's standards (Acts 2:38; 3:19).

Jesus died, but He did not remain dead. After three days, God's Spirit miraculously raised Him to life again. God's Spirit does something similar in us. When we receive Jesus as our sacrifice and repent of our sins, our hearts are changed. We become spiritually alive! We develop new desires and attitudes (2 Corinthians 5:17). We begin to make choices that please God (1 John 3:9). If we do fail and commit sins, we can ask God for forgiveness. "If we confess our sins, he is faithful and just to forgive us our sins, and to cleanse us from all unrighteousness" (1 John 1:9).

Once our hearts have been changed, we want to continue growing spiritually. We will be happy to let Jesus be the Master of our lives and will want to become more like Him. To do this, we must meditate on God's Word and commune with God in prayer. We will testify to others of this change by being baptized and sharing the good news of God's victory over sin and death. Fellowship with a faithful group of believers will strengthen our walk with God (1 John 1:7).